THE BEATLES FOR U[illegible]E

Arranged by Barrett Tagliarino

ISBN 978-1-4234-3013-1

7777 W. Bluemound Rd. P.O. Box 13819 Milwaukee, WI 53213

Visit Hal Leonard Online at
www.halleonard.com

PREFACE

Welcome to *The Beatles for Ukulele*! Unlike many books of this type, each arrangement in this book includes *every* measure of the song, as it was originally recorded—nothing is left out. So if you want to play along with the recorded versions, all you have to do is follow the repeat signs and any D.C. or D.S. instructions. And when you come to instrumental sections, the chords are provided so you can keep strumming your uke.

All songs are arranged for the standard "My Dog Has Fleas" ukulele tuning: G–C–E–A. However, sometimes the Beatles altered the speed of tape machines during the recording process, producing results that were not always exactly at concert pitch (A440). So you may need to slightly adjust your tuning (by an eighth or quarter step up or down) for a few of the songs in this book in case you wish to play along with the original recordings.

Now let's join in with the Fab Four on some of the greatest pop songs ever written!

Barrett Tagliarino

CONTENTS

All My Loving

Words and Music by John Lennon and Paul McCartney

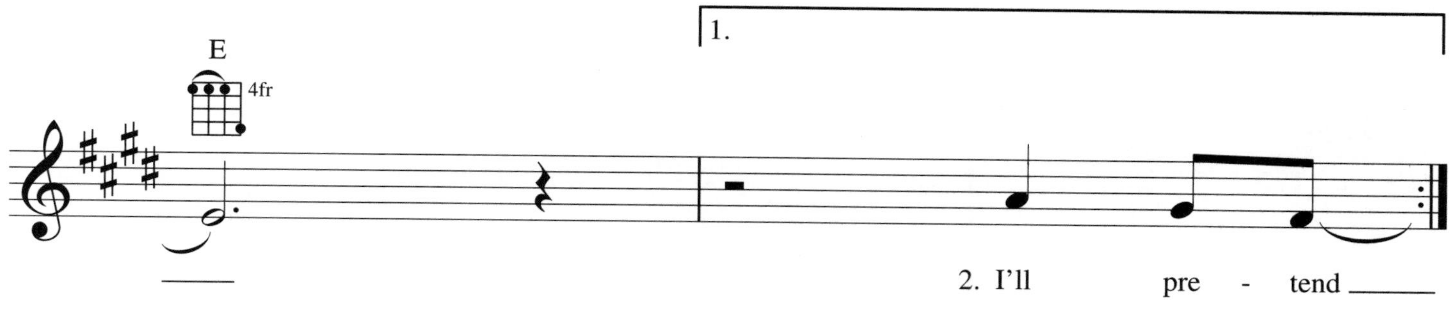
E
4fr
1.
2. I'll pre - tend

2.
Chorus
C♯m
4fr
C+
3fr
3
All my lov - ing I will send to you

E
C♯m
4fr
All my lov - ing, darl -

To Coda
C+
3fr
E
- ing I'll be true.

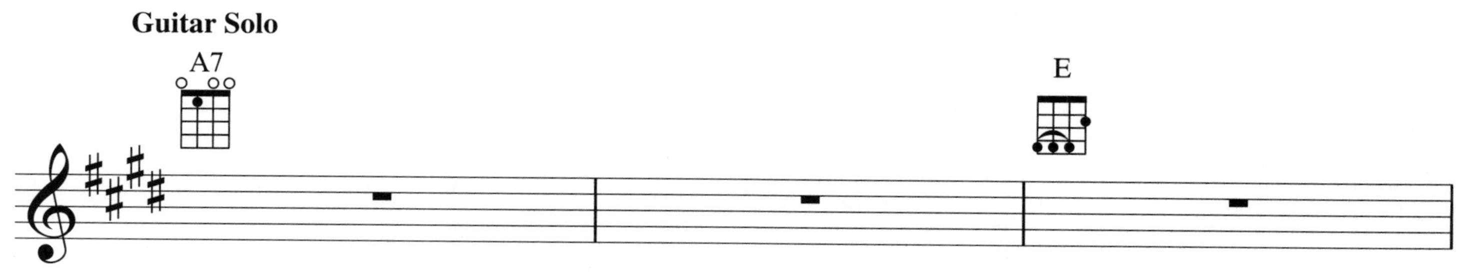
Guitar Solo
A7
E

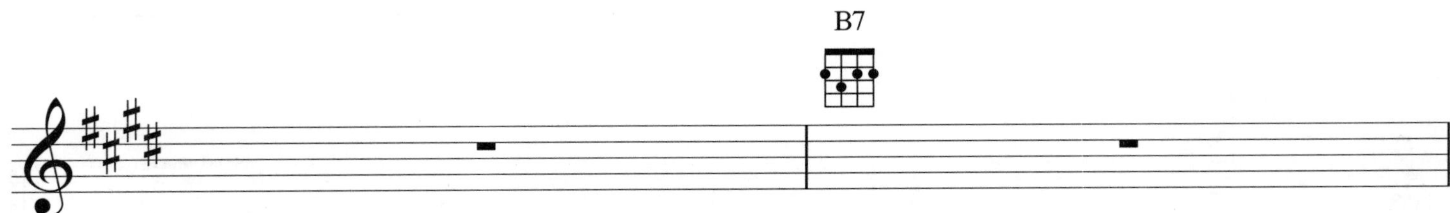
B7

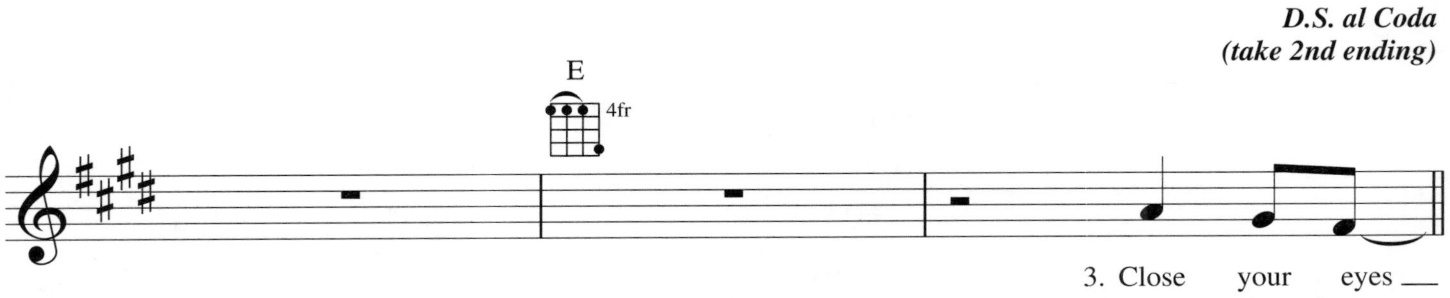
D.S. al Coda
(take 2nd ending)
E
4fr
3. Close your eyes

Coda
Outro
E
C♯m
4fr
All my lov - ing,
all my

E
C♯m
4fr
lov - ing,
ooh,
all my
lov - ing,

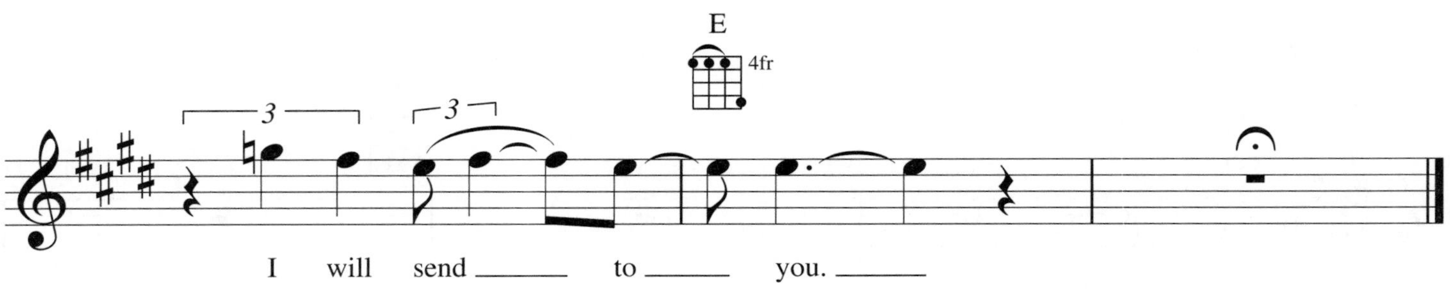
E
4fr
I will send to you.

All You Need Is Love

Words and Music by John Lennon and Paul McCartney

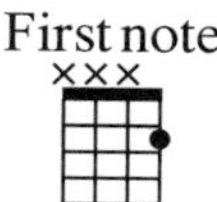

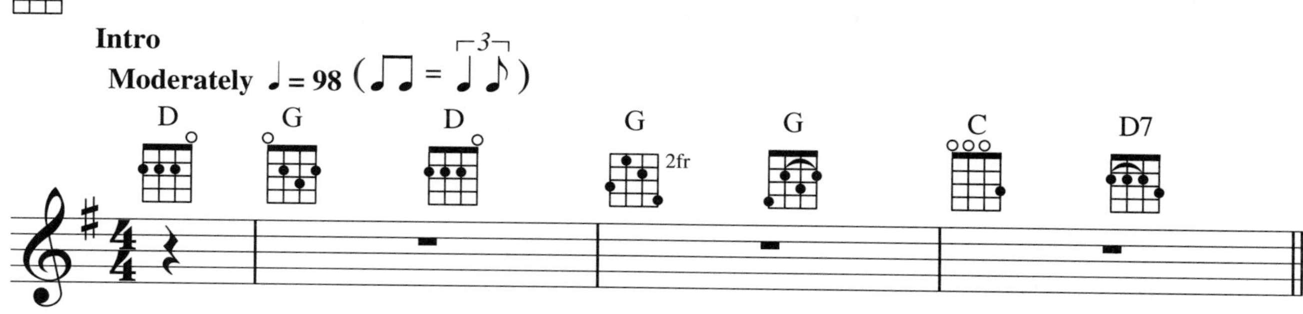

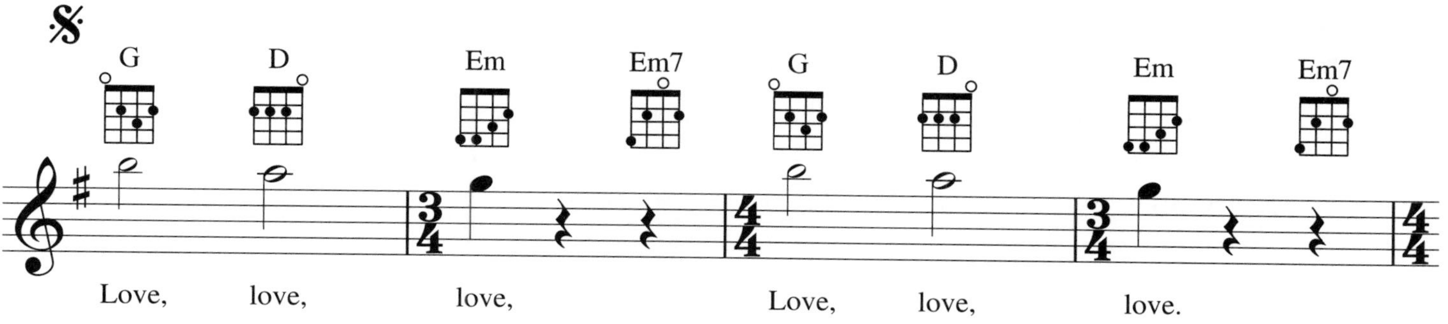

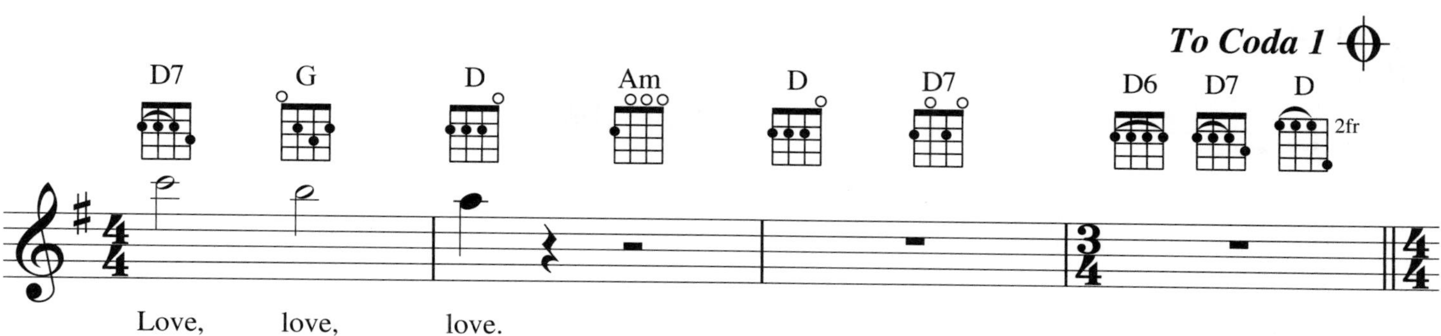

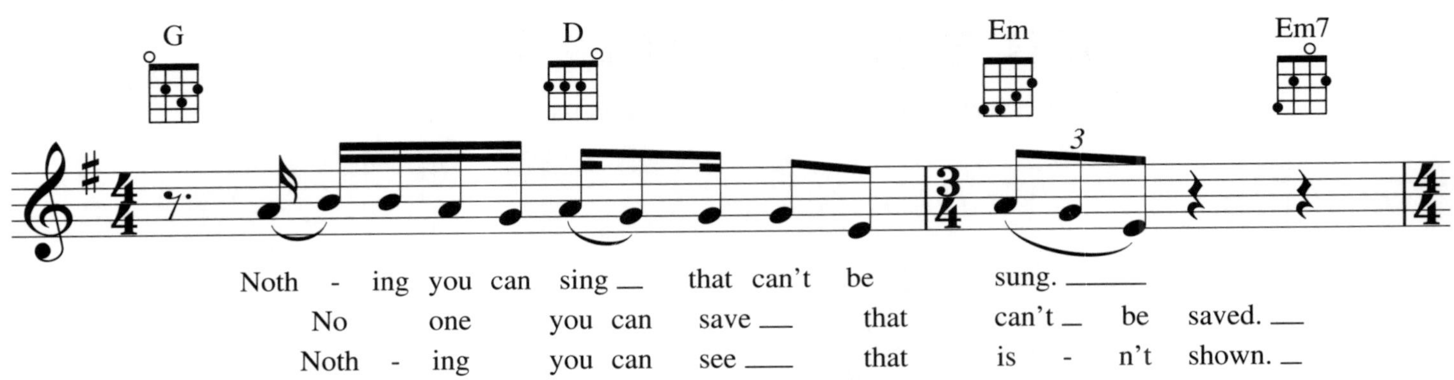
G
D
Em
Em7
3
Noth - ing you can sing that can't be sung.
No one you can save that can't be saved.
Noth - ing you can see that is - n't shown.

D7
G
D
Am
Noth - ing you can say, but you can learn how to play the game.
No - thing you can do, but you can learn how to be you in time.
There's no - where you can be that is - n't where you're meant to be.
It's

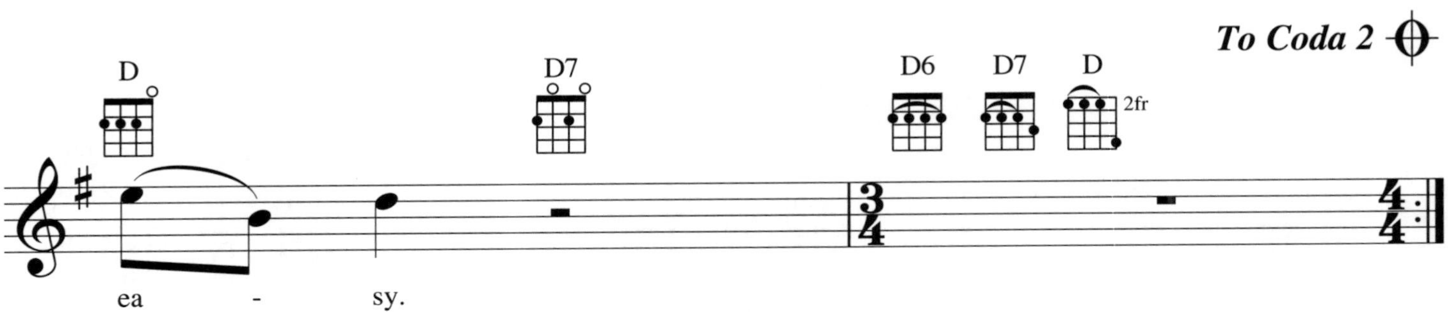
To Coda 2
D
D7
D6
D7
D
2fr
ea - sy.

Chorus
G
A
D
All you need is love.

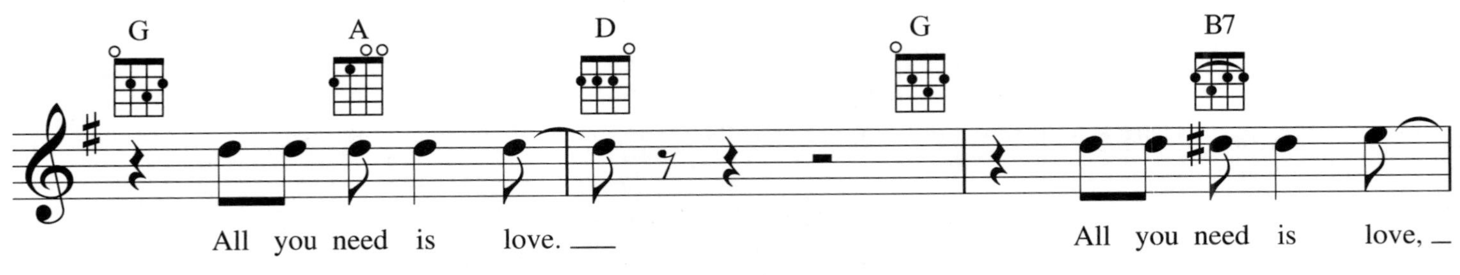
G
A
D
G
B7
All you need is love.
All you need is love,

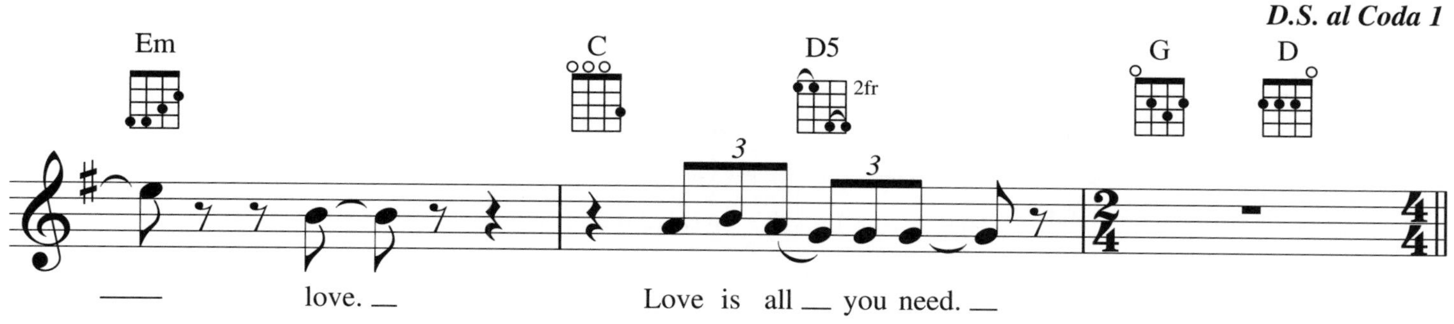

D.S. al Coda 1
Em
C
D5
2fr
G
D
love.
Love is all you need.

Coda 1
G
A
D
G
All you need is love.

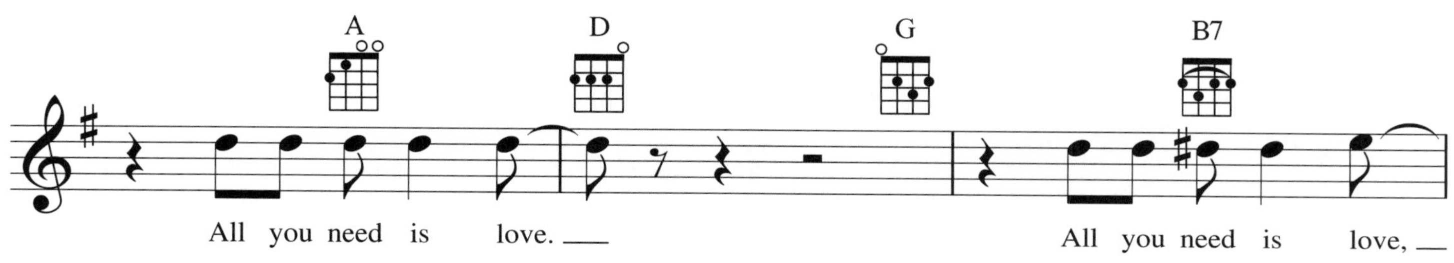

A
D
G
B7
All you need is love.
All you need is love,

D.S.S. al Coda 2
(no repeat)
Em
Em7
C
D
G
love.
Love is all you need.

Coda 2
Chorus
G
A
D
All you need is love.

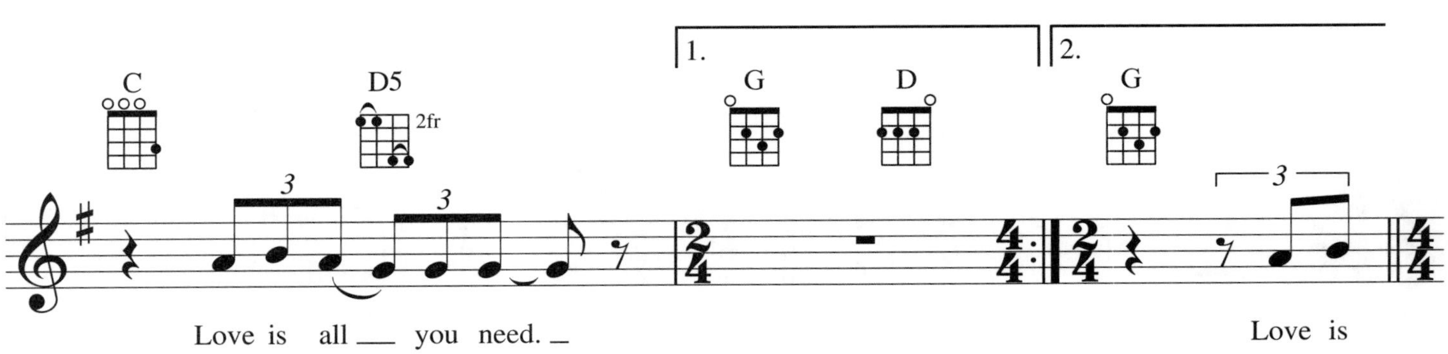

Outro

Play 12 times and fade

And I Love Her

Words and Music by John Lennon and Paul McCartney

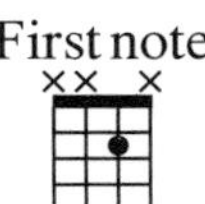

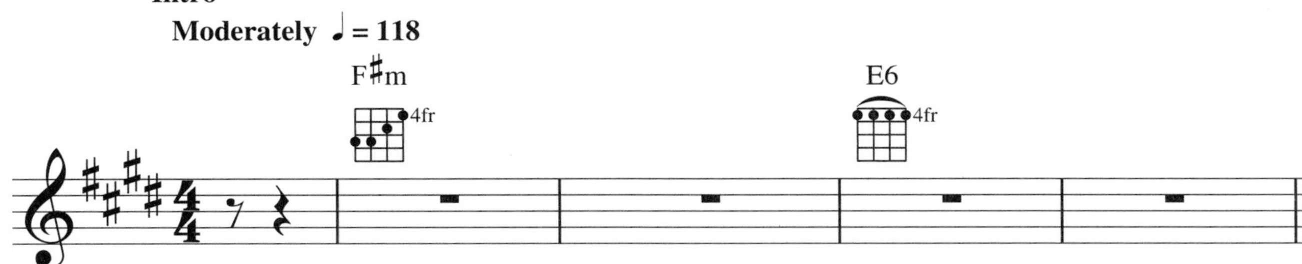

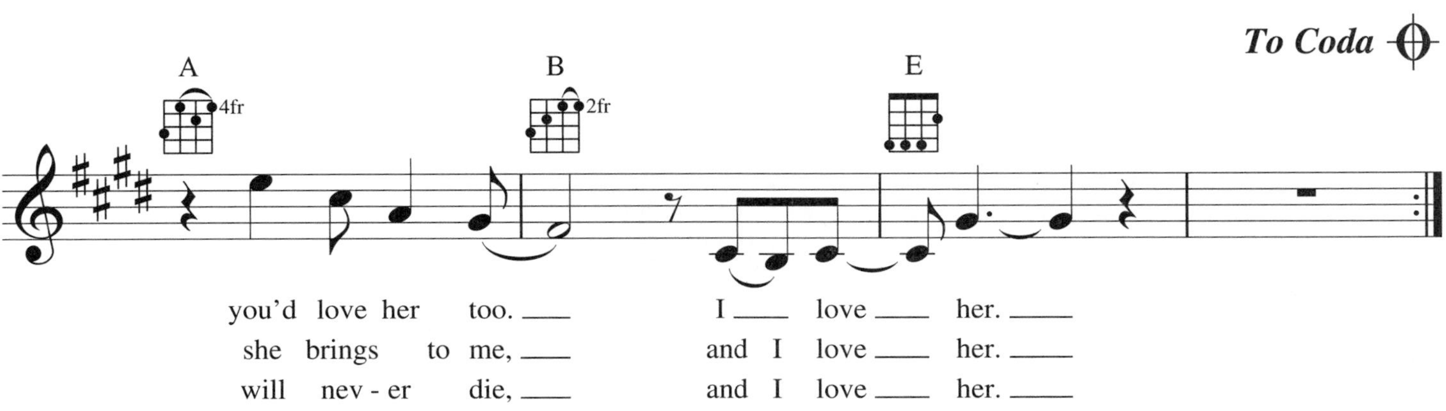

Bridge

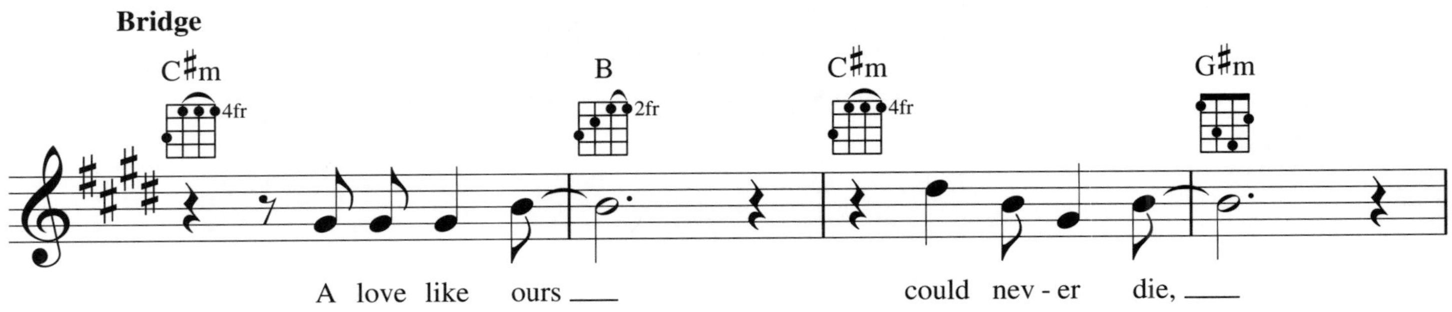

D.S. al Coda
(no repeat)

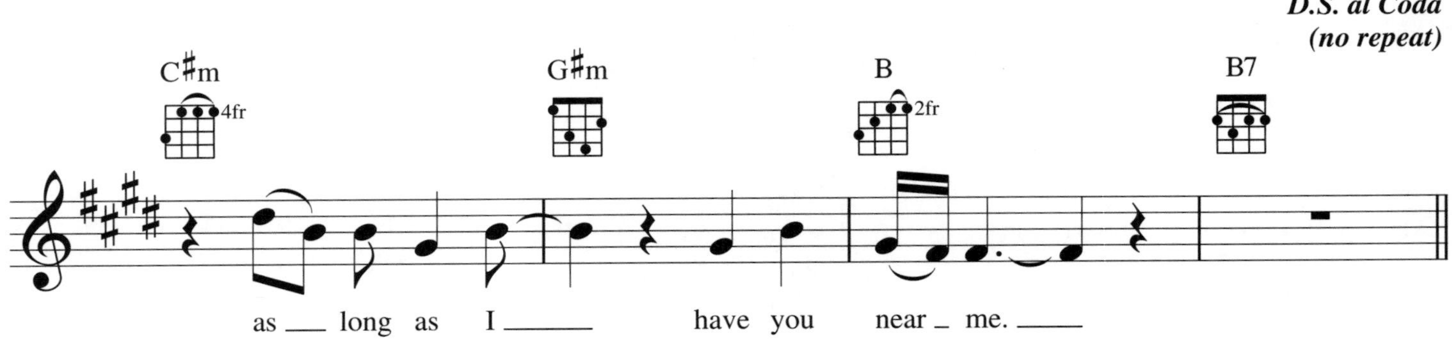

Coda

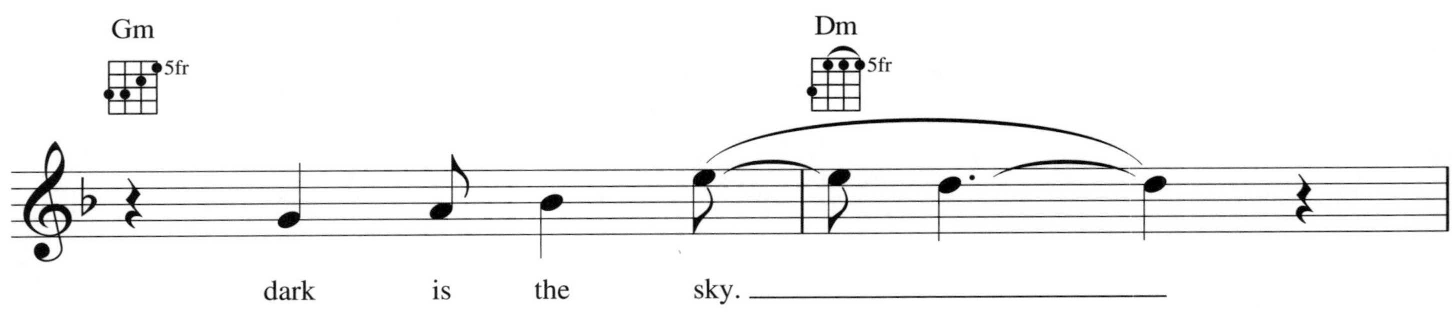

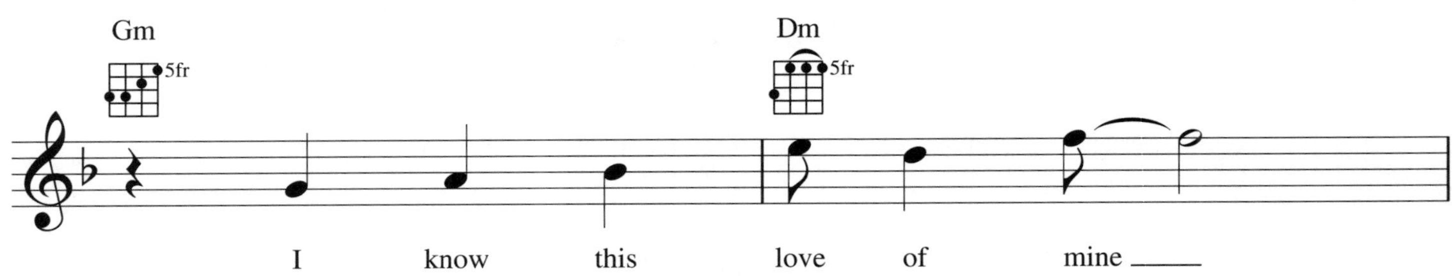

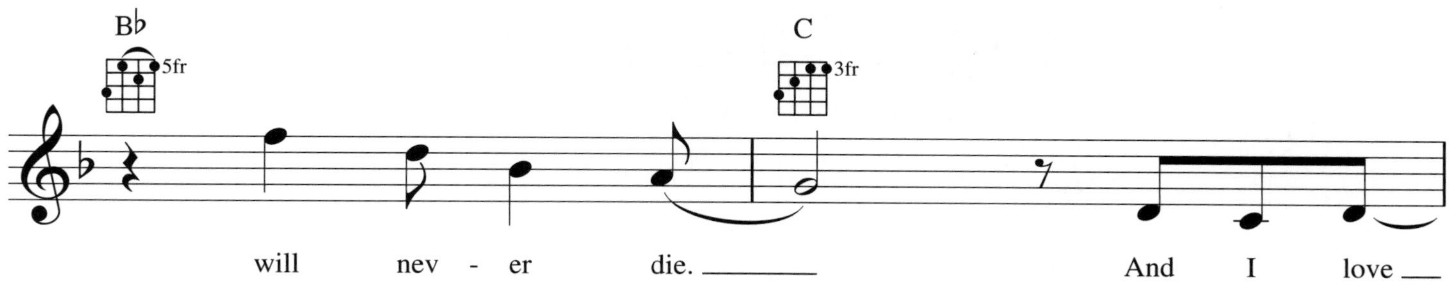
B♭
5fr
C
3fr
will nev - er die.
And I love

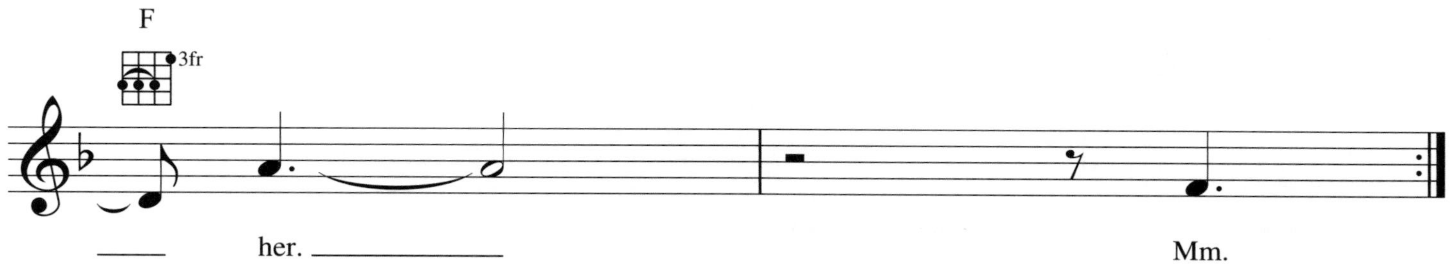
F
3fr
her.
Mm.

Outro

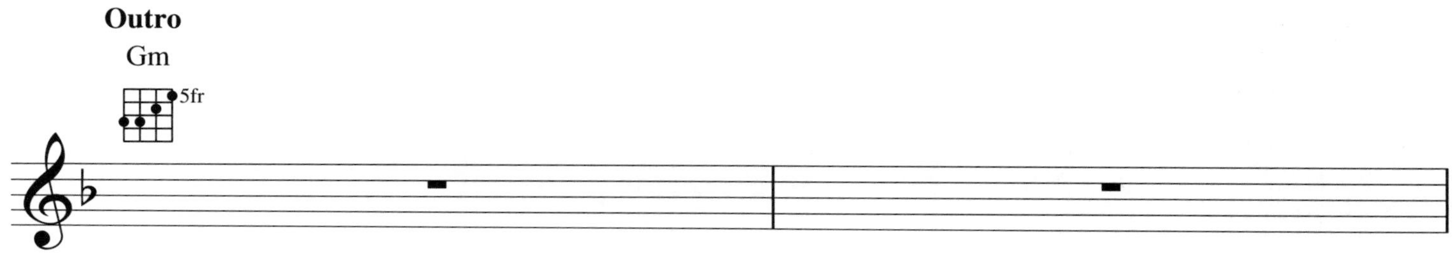
Gm
5fr

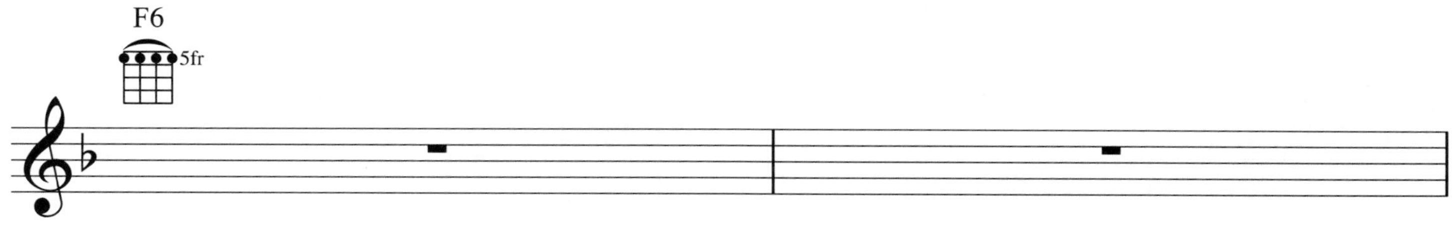
F6
5fr

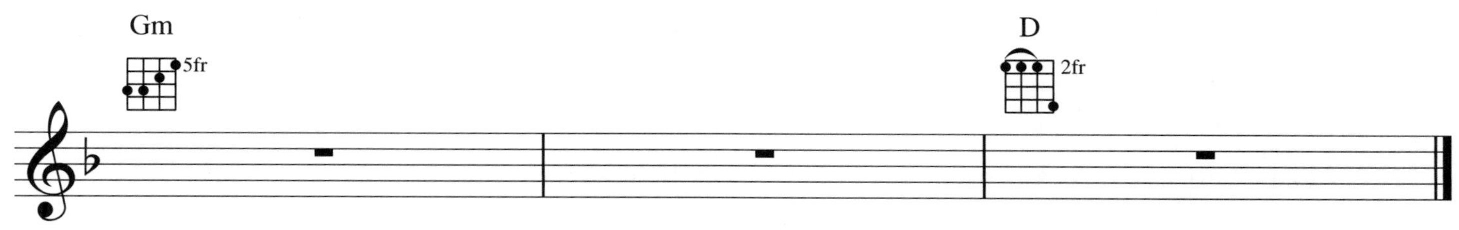
Gm
5fr
D
2fr

Eight Days a Week

To Coda
D
E
4fr
G
D
ain't got noth - in' but love,
1., 3., 4. babe,
2. girl,
eight days a week.

Bridge
A
Bm
Eight days a week,
I love
you.

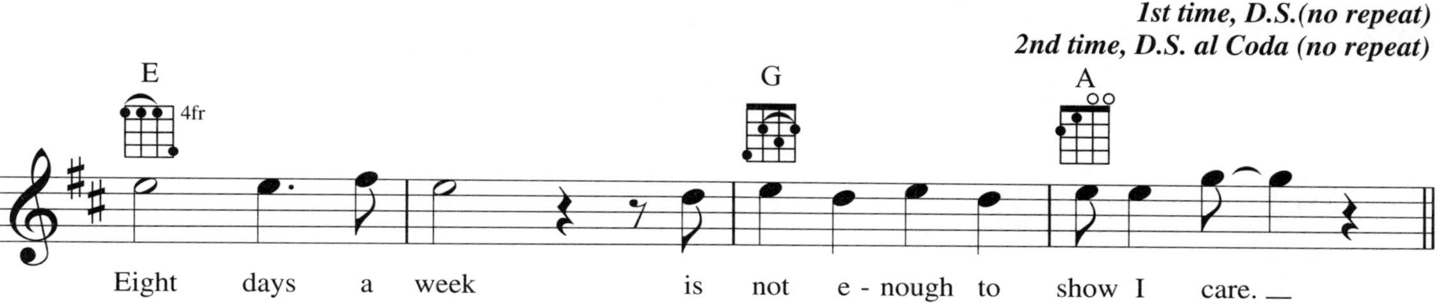
1st time, D.S.(no repeat)
2nd time, D.S. al Coda (no repeat)
E
4fr
G
A
Eight days a week
is not e - nough to show I care.

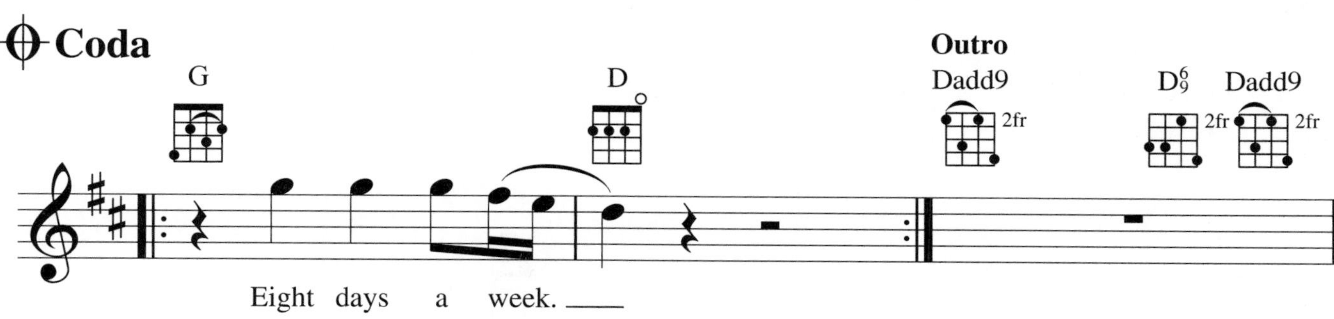
Coda
G
D
Outro
Dadd9
2fr
D6/9
2fr
Dadd9
2fr
Eight days a week.

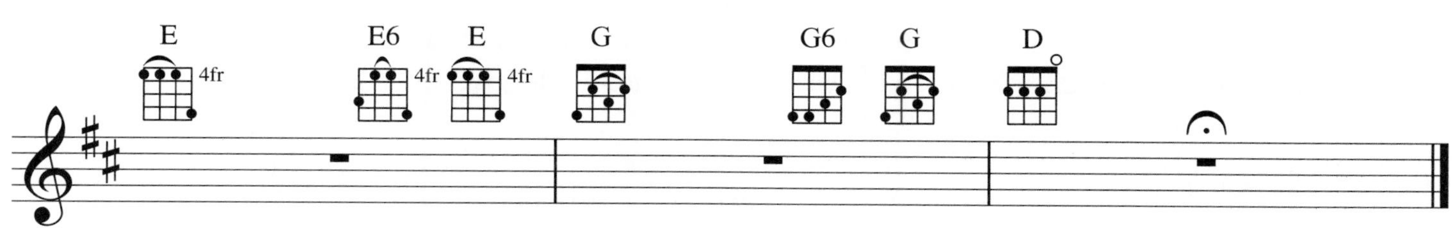
E
4fr
E6
4fr
E
4fr
G
G6
G
D

Can't Buy Me Love

Words and Music by John Lennon and Paul McCartney

Intro-Chorus

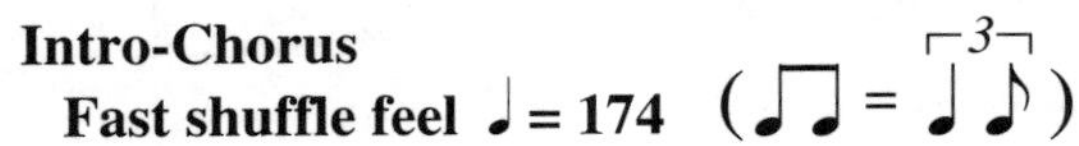

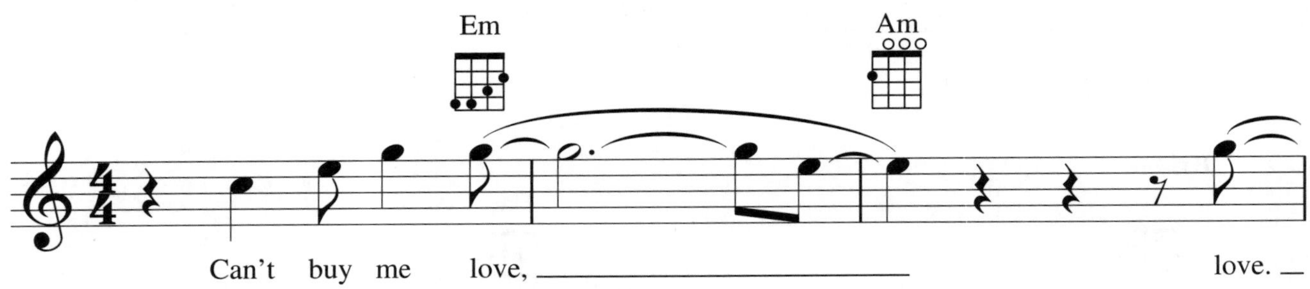

Verse

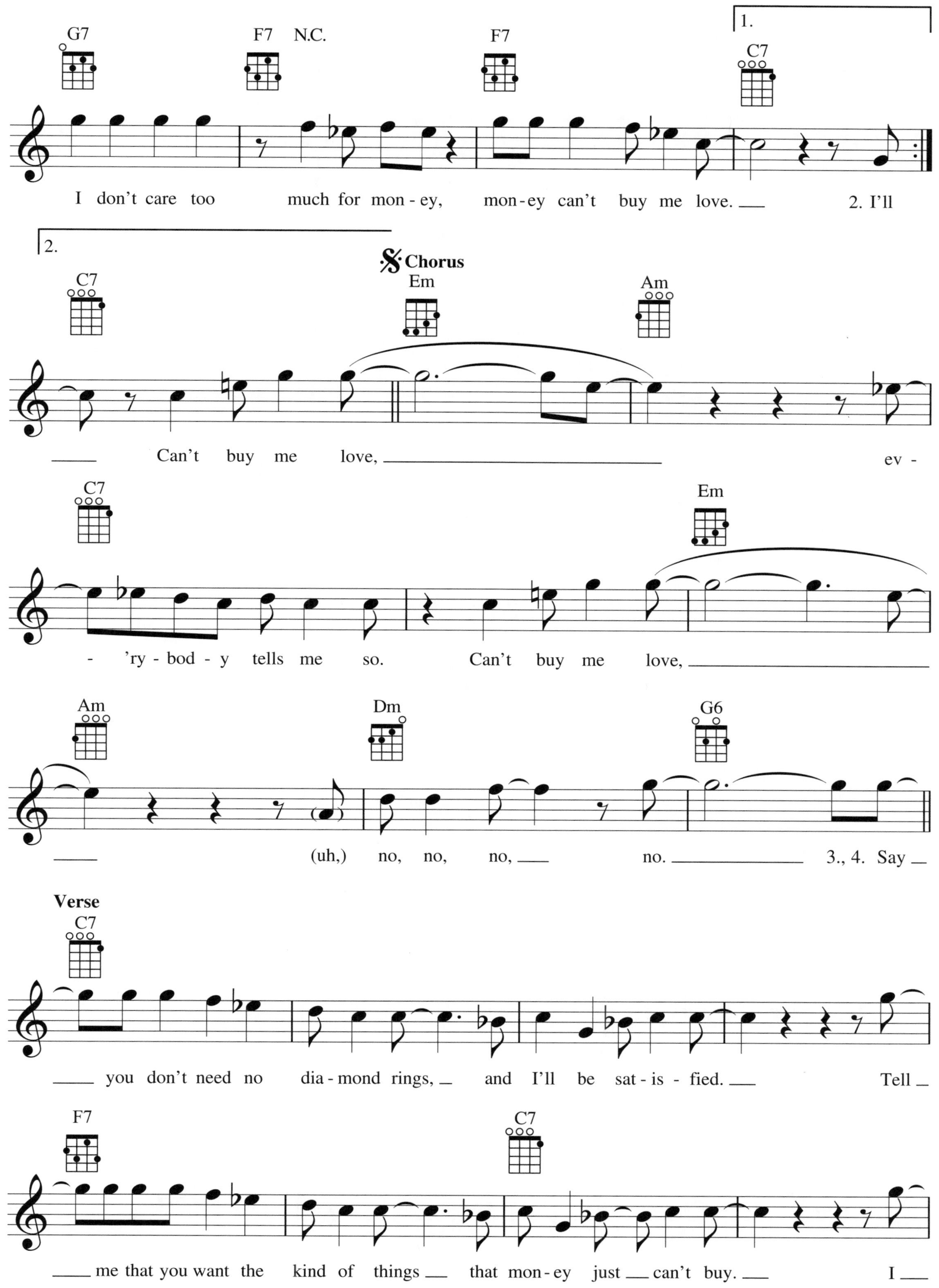
G7
F7 N.C.
F7
1.
C7
I don't care too much for mon-ey, mon-ey can't buy me love.
2. I'll
2.
C7
Chorus
Em
Am
Can't buy me love,
ev-'ry-bod-y tells me so.
C7
Em
Can't buy me love,
Am
Dm
G6
(uh,) no, no, no, no.
3., 4. Say
Verse
C7
you don't need no dia-mond rings, and I'll be sat-is-fied.
Tell
F7
C7
me that you want the kind of things that mon-ey just can't buy.
I

To Coda
G7
F7 N.C.
F7
don't care too much for mon - ey, mon - ey can't buy me love.
Guitar Solo
C7
G7
C7
scream: Ow!
F7
C7
G7
F7
C7
D.S. al Coda
Hey! Can't buy me love
Coda
F7
C7
Chorus
Em
Am
mon - ey can't buy me love. Can't buy me love, love.
Em
Am
Dm
G6
C7
Can't buy me love, oh.

Good Day Sunshine

Words and Music by John Lennon and Paul McCartney

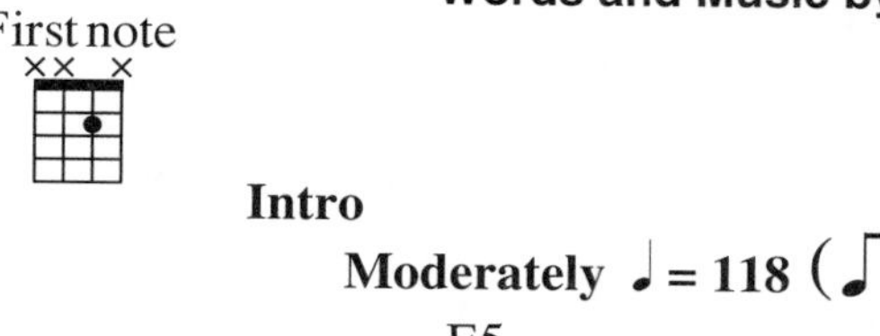

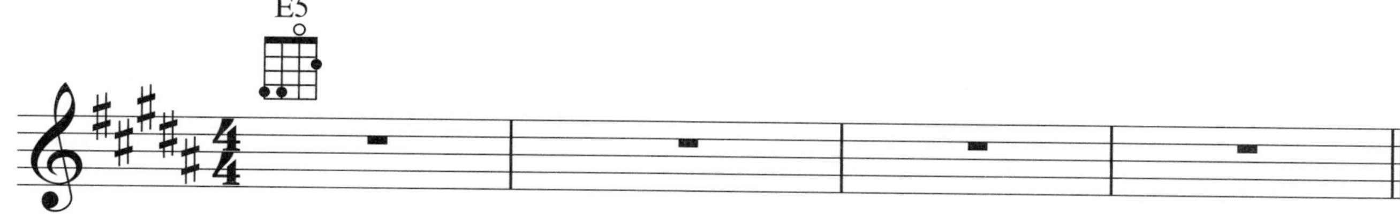

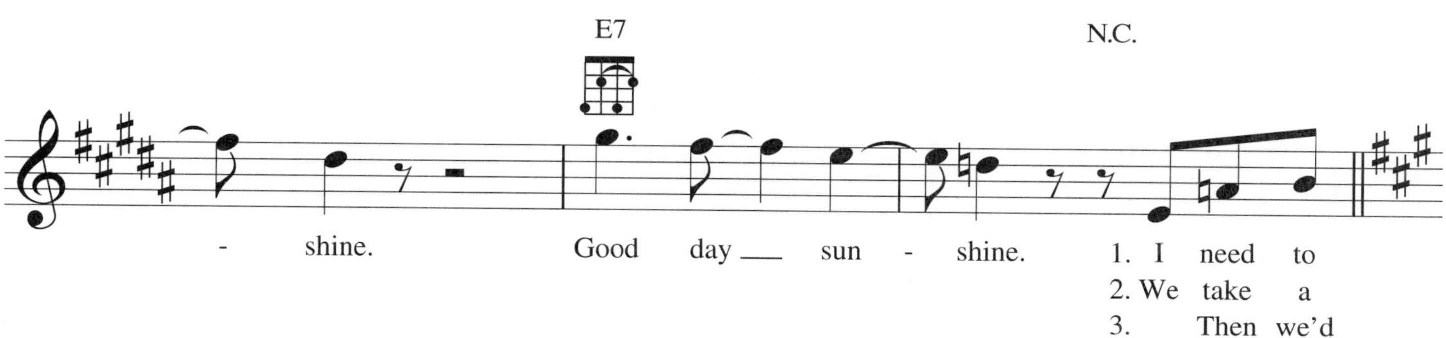

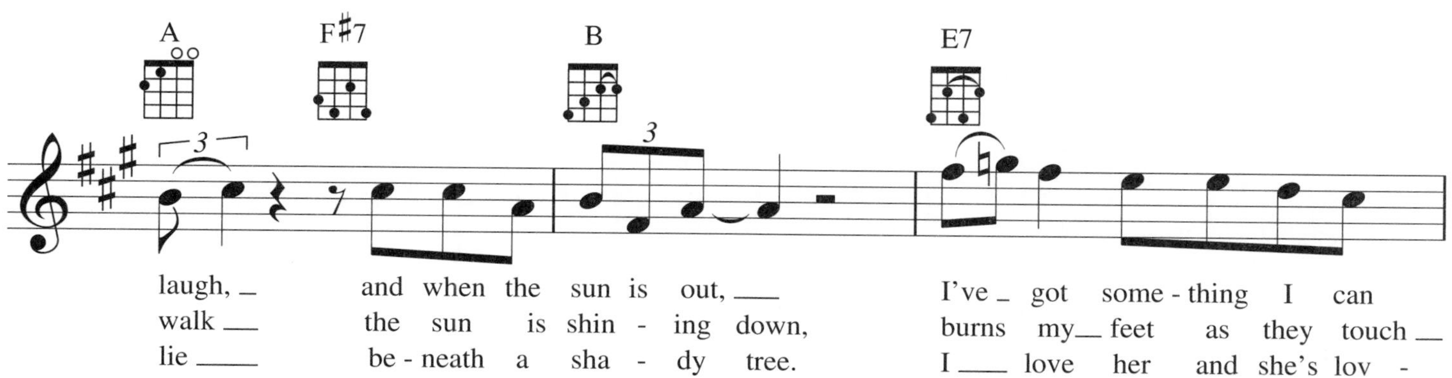

1.
A
F♯7
B
laugh a - bout. I feel good in a spe - cial way.
the ground.
ing me. She feels good. She knows she's look - ing fine.

E7
A
To Coda
I'm in love an' it's a sun - ny day.
I'm so proud to know that she is mine.

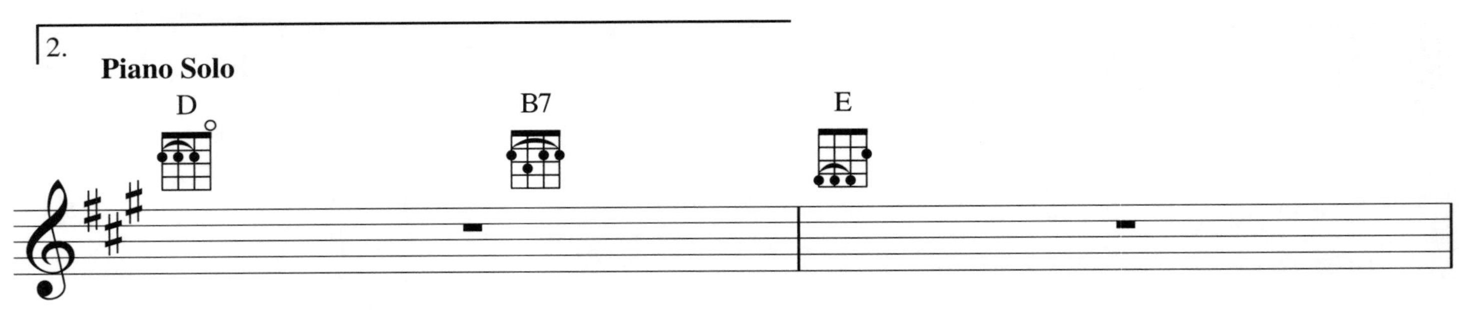
2.
Piano Solo
D
B7
E

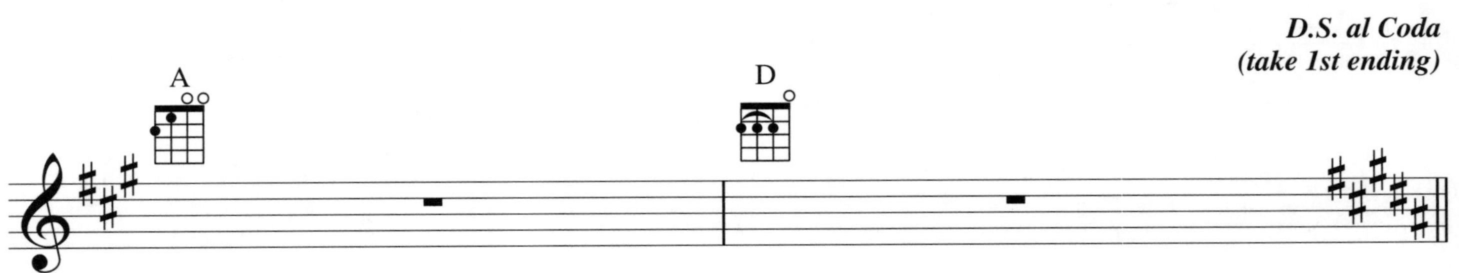
D.S. al Coda
(take 1st ending)
A
D

Coda

Chorus
B
F♯
Good day sun - shine.

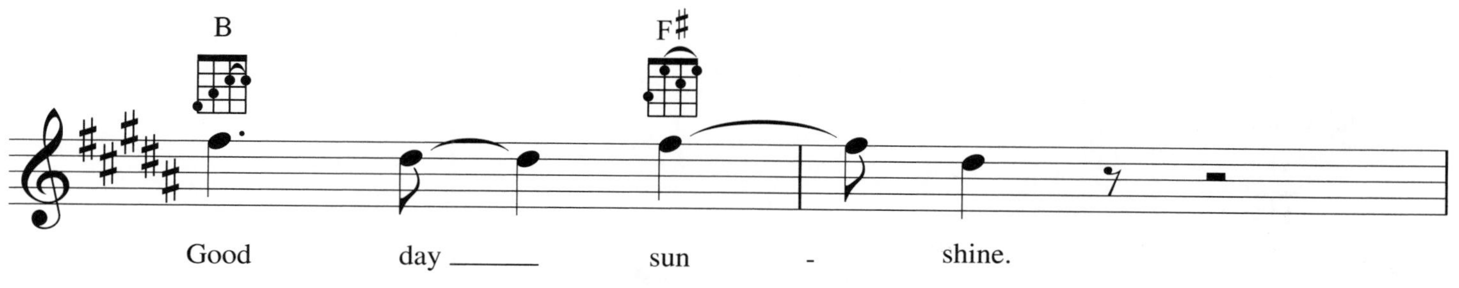
B
F♯
Good day sun - shine.

E
E7
F9
Good day sun - shine.
Good day sun -

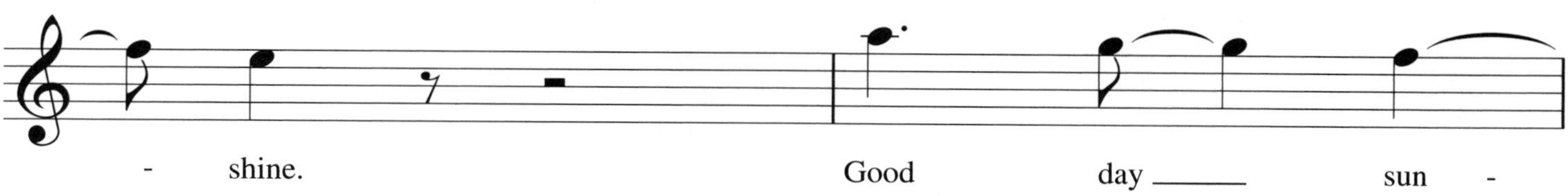
- shine.
Good day sun -

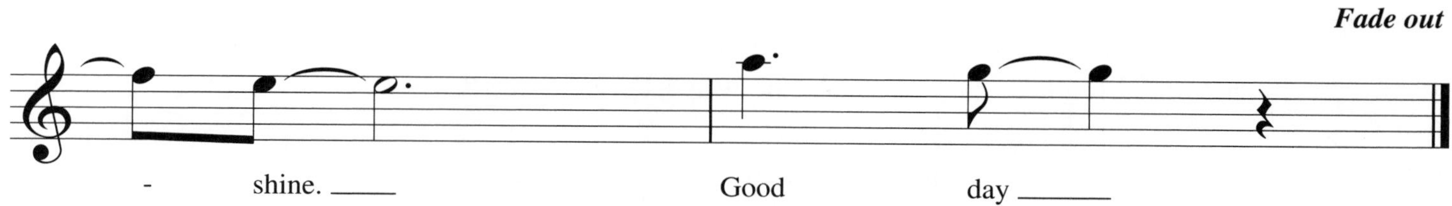
Fade out
- shine.
Good day

Got to Get You into My Life

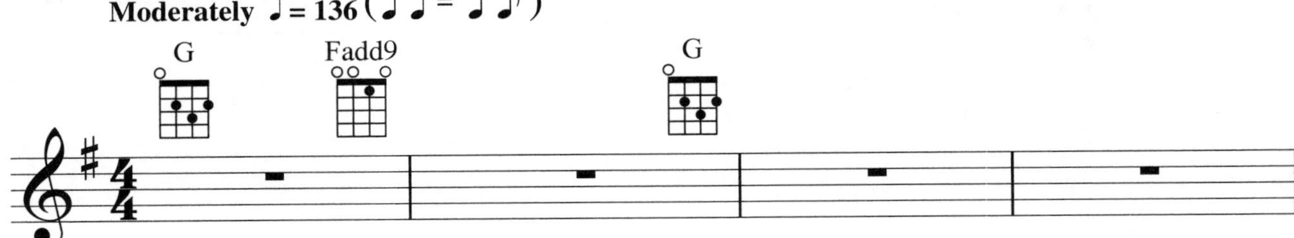

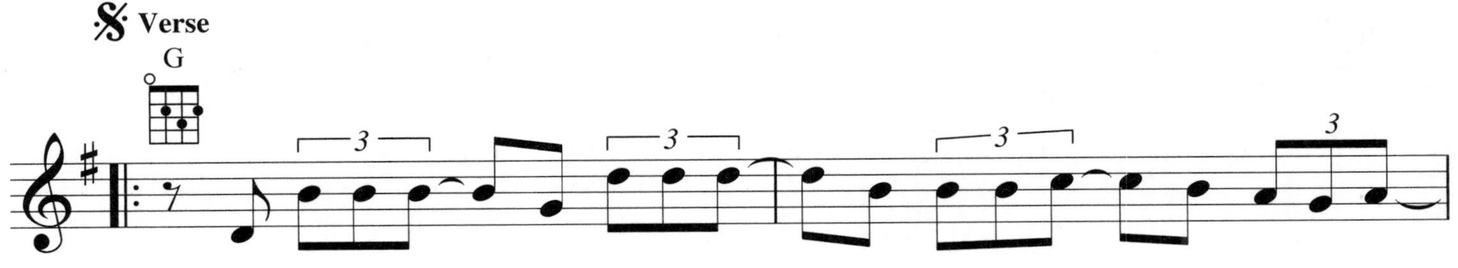

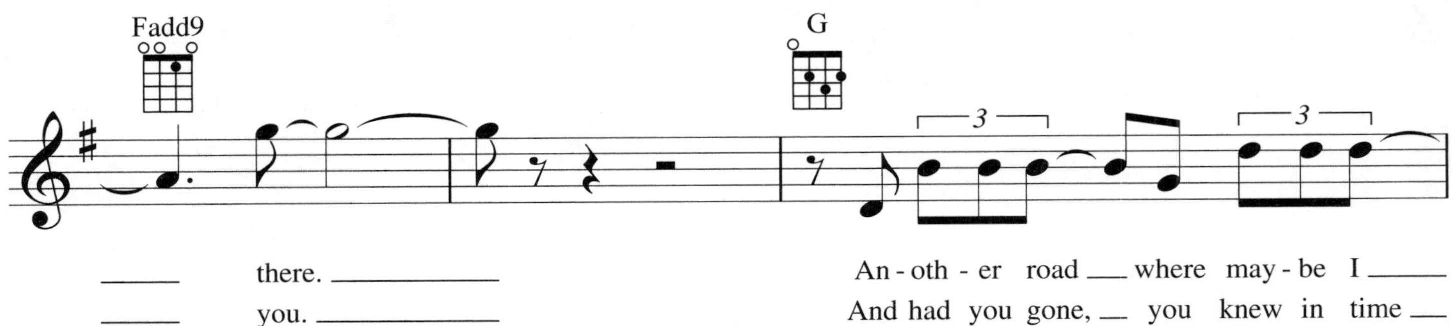

Bm
Bm(maj7)
Bm7
Bm6
Ooh, then I sud - den - ly see you. Ooh,
Ooh, you were meant to be near me. Ooh,
Ooh, then I sud - den - ly see you. Ooh,
Bm
Bm(maj7)
Bm7
Bm6
C
5fr
Cmaj7
5fr
did I tell you I need you ev - 'ry sin - gle
an' I want you to hear me. Say we'll be to -
did I tell you I need you ev - 'ry sin - gle
To Coda
1.
2.
Am7
5fr
D
2fr
G
day of my life?
geth - er ev - 'ry day.
day of my life?
Chorus
G
C
Got to get you in - to my life!
D
2fr
N.C.
G
D.S. al Coda

Coda
Chorus
G
C
Got to get you in - to my life!
D
2fr
G
Fadd9
I
G
C
got to get you in - to my life!
D N.C.
2fr
G
Verse
G
3
3
3
4. I was a - lone, I took a ride, I did - n't know

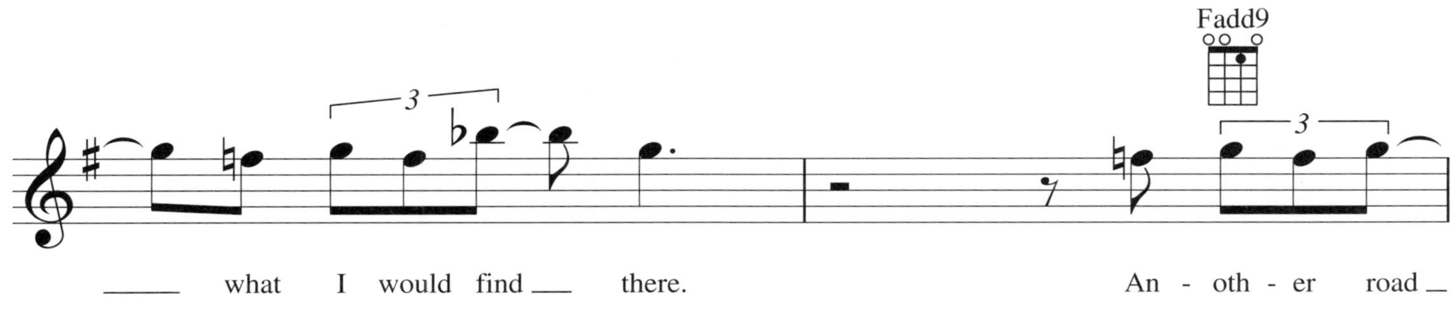
Fadd9
3
what I would find there.
An - oth - er road

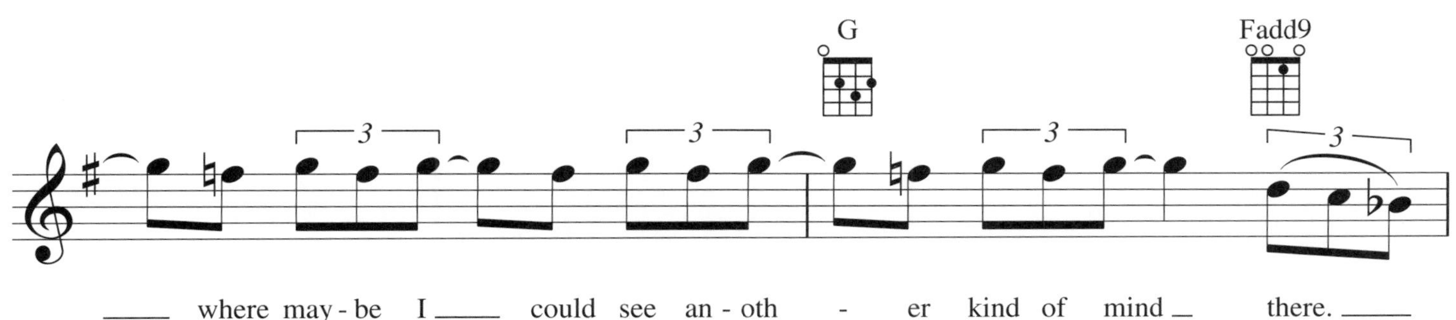
G
Fadd9
3
where may - be I could see an - oth - er kind of mind there.

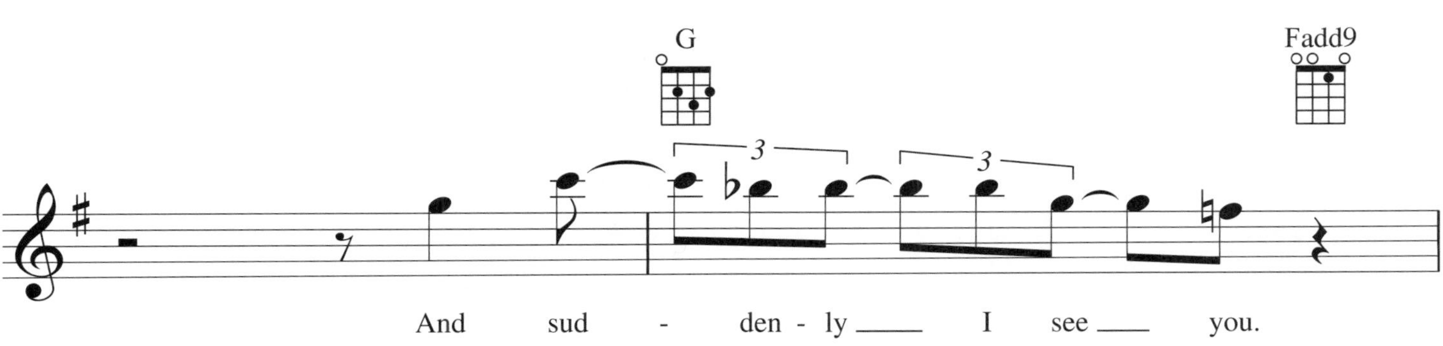
G
Fadd9
3
And sud - den - ly I see you.

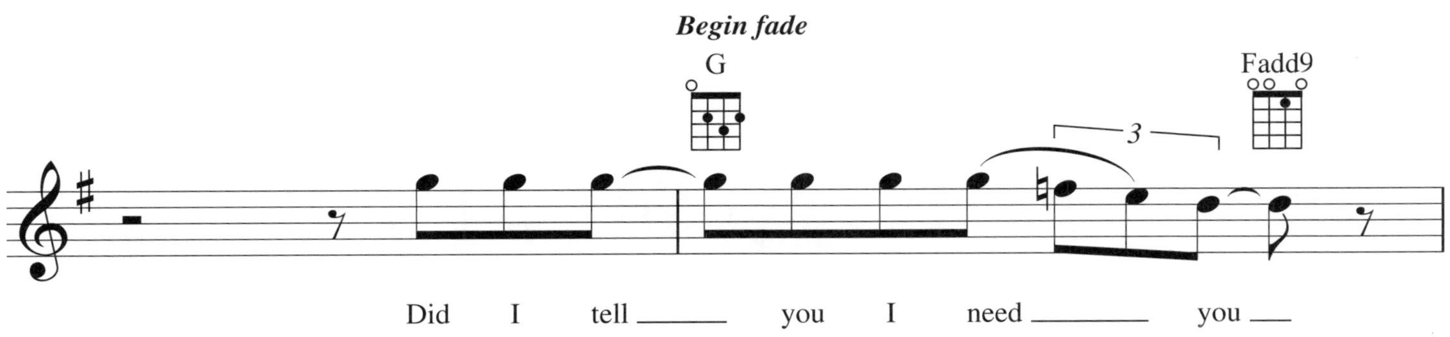
Begin fade
G
Fadd9
3
Did I tell you I need you

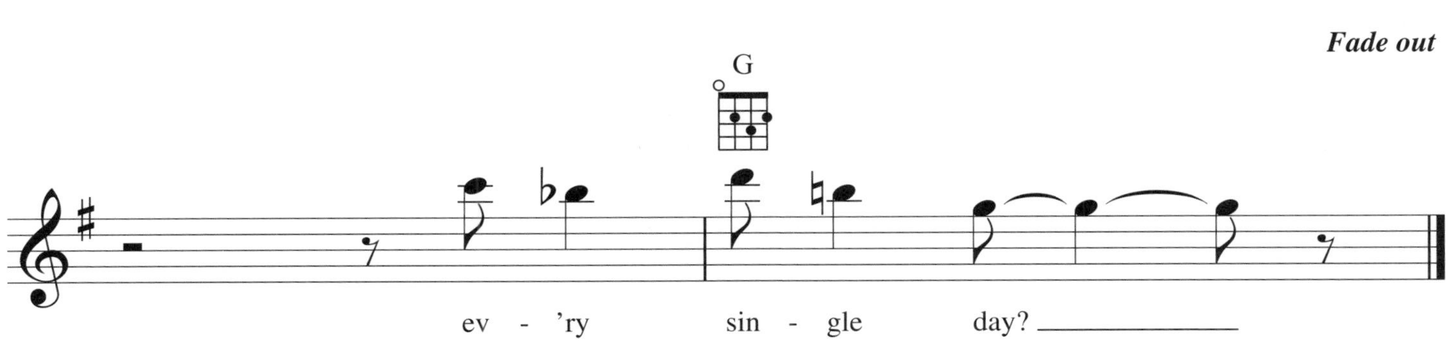
Fade out
G
ev - 'ry sin - gle day?

Here Comes the Sun

Words and Music by George Harrison

First note

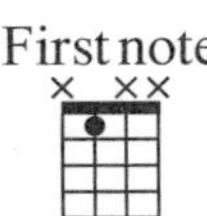

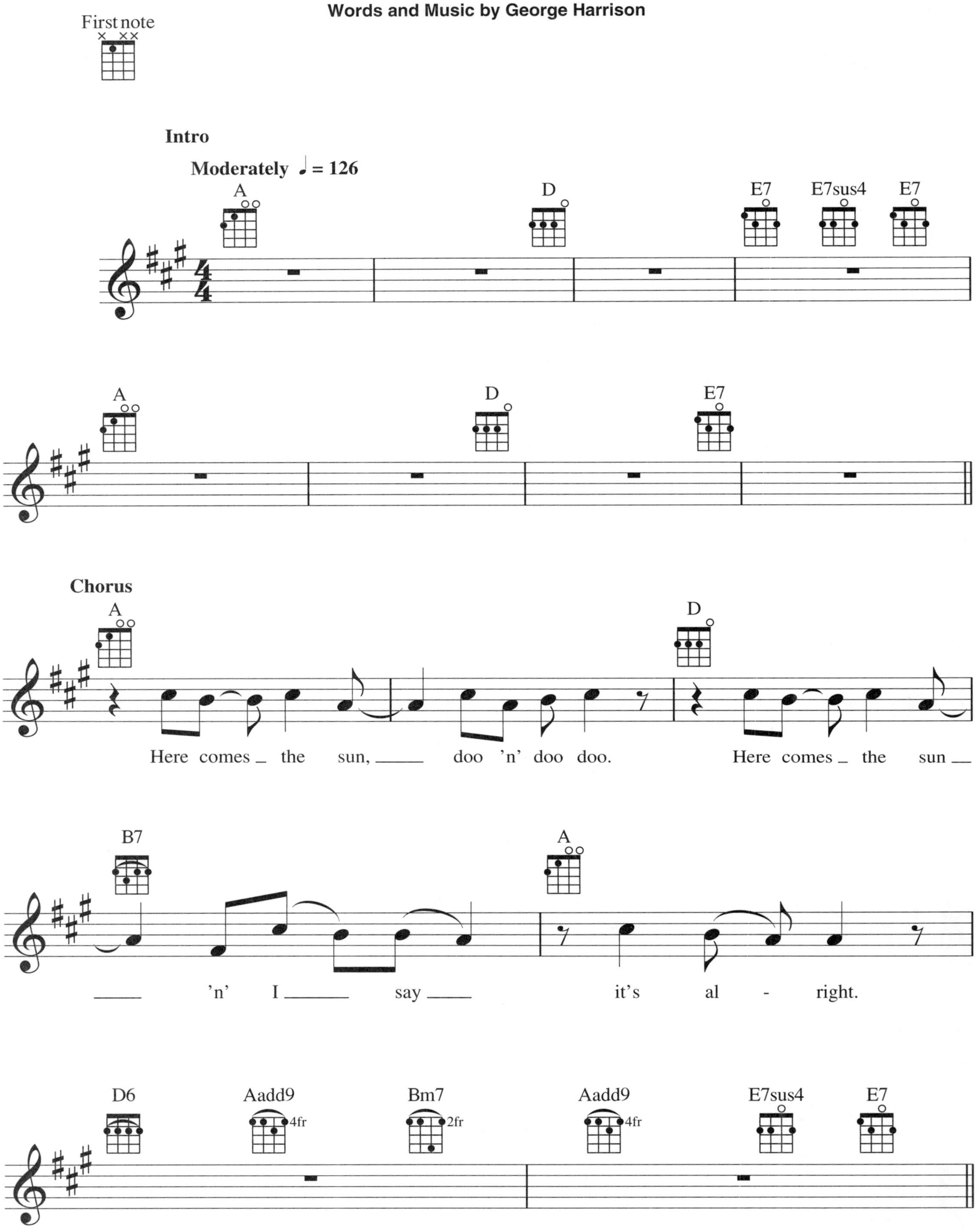
Intro
Moderately ♩ = 126
A D E7 E7sus4 E7
A D E7
Chorus
A D
Here comes the sun, doo 'n' doo doo. Here comes the sun
B7 A
'n' I say it's al - right.
D6 Aadd9 Bm7 Aadd9 E7sus4 E7
2fr
4fr

Verse
A
D
1. Lit - tle dar - lin', it's been a long,
2. Lit - tle dar - lin', the smiles re - turn -
3. Lit - tle dar - lin', I feel that ice
E7
E7sus4
E7
cold, lone - ly win - ter.
- ing to their fac - es
is slow - ly melt - ing.
A
D
Lit - tle dar - lin', it feels like years
Lit - tle dar - lin', it seems like years
Lit - tle dar - lin', it seems like years
E7
E7sus4
since it's been here.
since it's been here.
since it's been clear.
Chorus
A
D
Here comes the sun, doo 'n' doo doo. Here comes the sun

B7 A D6 Aadd9 Bm7
4fr 2fr
'n' I say it's al - right.
To Coda
Aadd9 E7sus4 E7 A
4fr
1.
E7 E7sus4 E7
2.
Bridge
E7 E
C G D
A E7 E C G
Sun, sun,
D A E7 E
sun, here it comes.
1., 2., 3.
C G D A E7 E
Sun, sun, sun, here it comes.

4.
D.S. al Coda
E7sus4
E7
E
Coda
A
Here comes the sun. (Doo 'n' doo doo.)
D
B7
A
Here comes the sun. It's al - right.
D6
Aadd9
4fr
Bm7
2fr
Aadd9
4fr
E7sus4
E7
A
It's al - right.
D6
Aadd9
4fr
Bm7
2fr
Aadd9
4fr
E7sus4
E7
C
G
D
A

Here, There and Everywhere

Words and Music by John Lennon and Paul McCartney

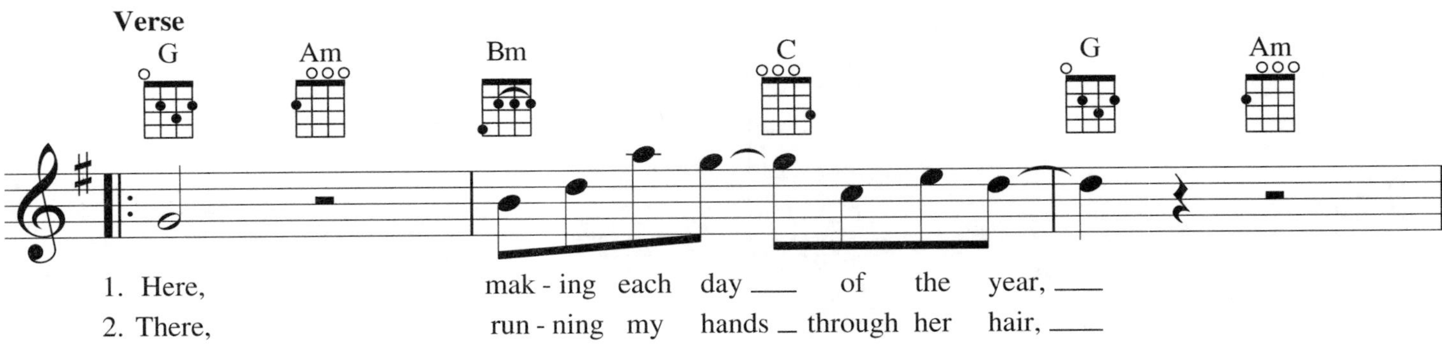

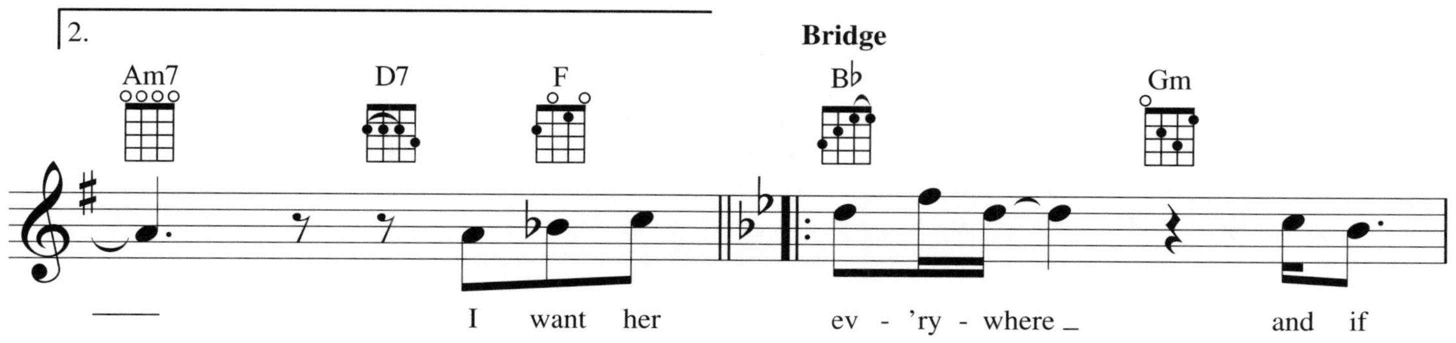
2.
Bridge
Am7
D7
F
B♭
Gm
I want her ev - 'ry - where and if
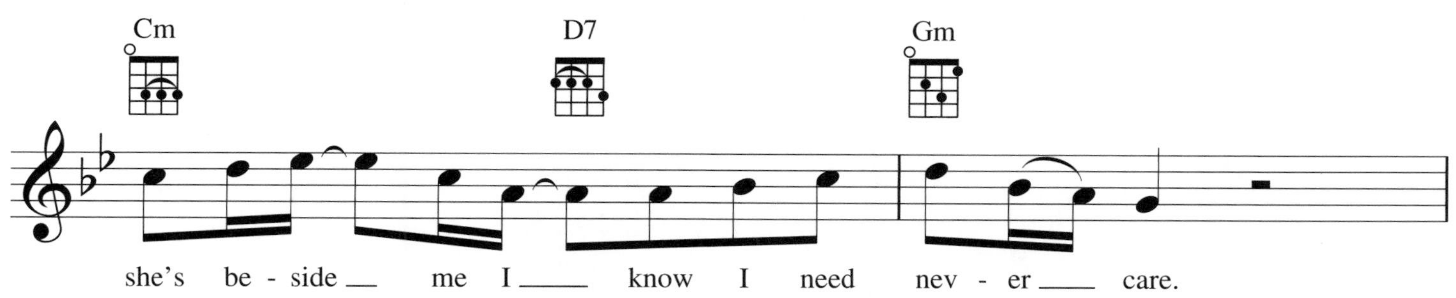
Cm
D7
Gm
she's be - side me I know I need nev - er care.

Verse
Cm
D7
G
Am
But to love her is to need her 3., 4. ev - 'ry - where,
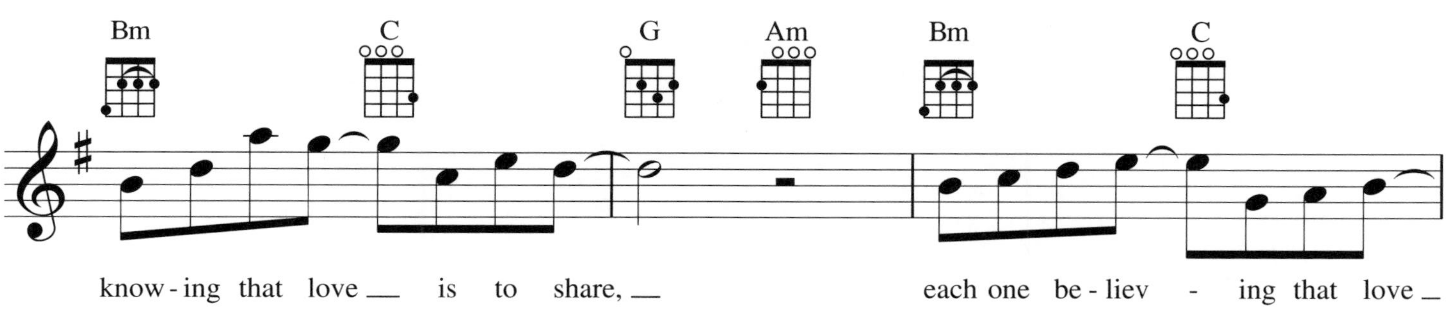
Bm
C
G
Am
Bm
C
know - ing that love is to share, each one be - liev - ing that love
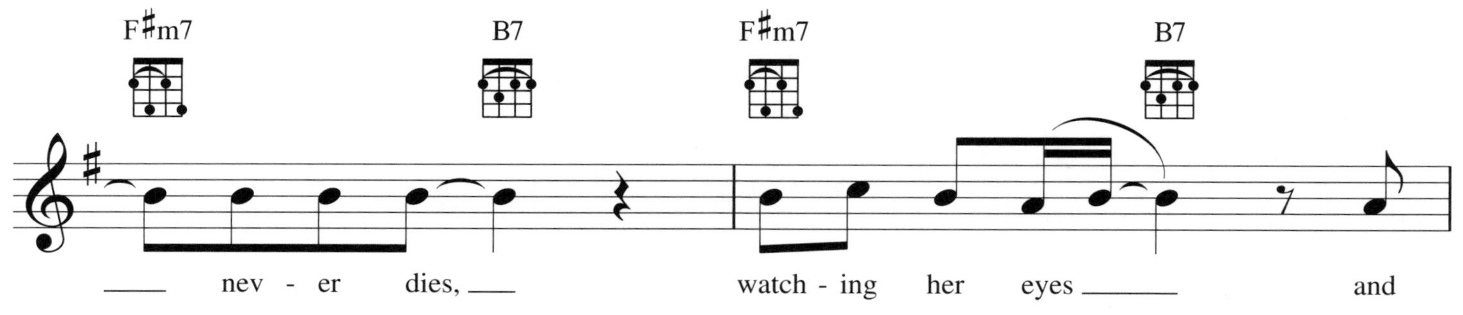
F♯m7
B7
F♯m7
B7
nev - er dies, watch - ing her eyes and

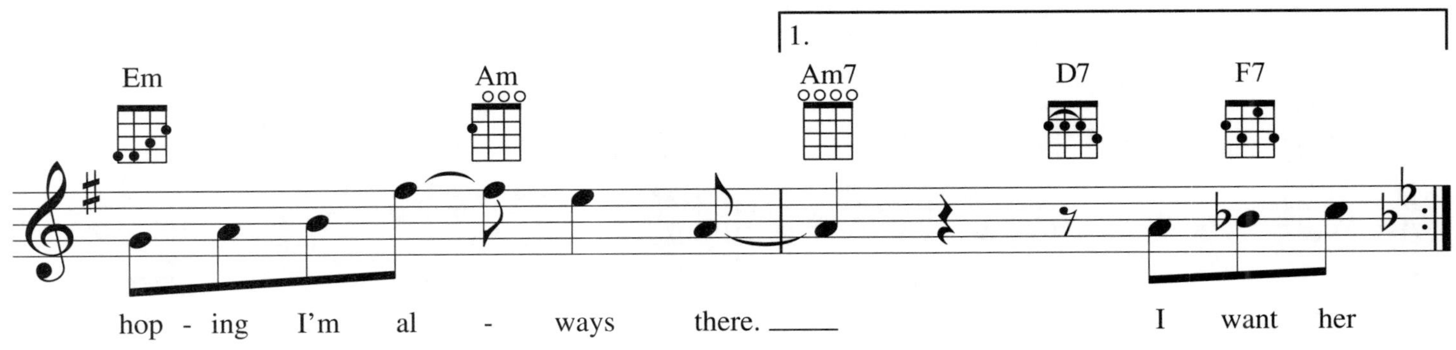
1.
Em
Am
Am7
D7
F7
hop - ing I'm al - ways there.
I want her

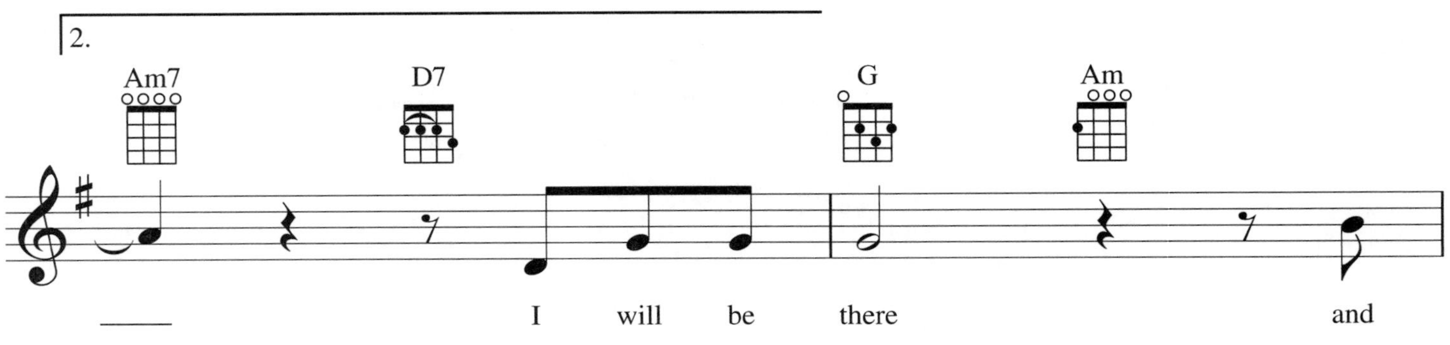
2.
Am7
D7
G
Am
I will be there
and

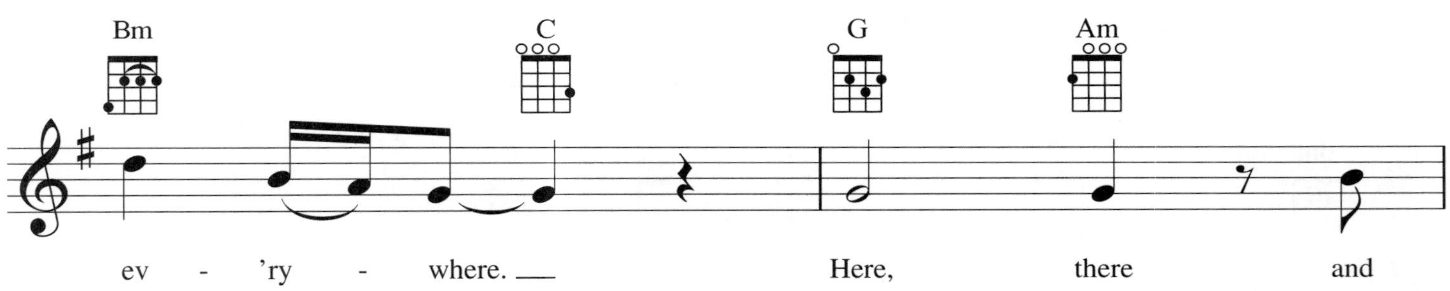
Bm
C
G
Am
ev - 'ry - where.
Here, there
and

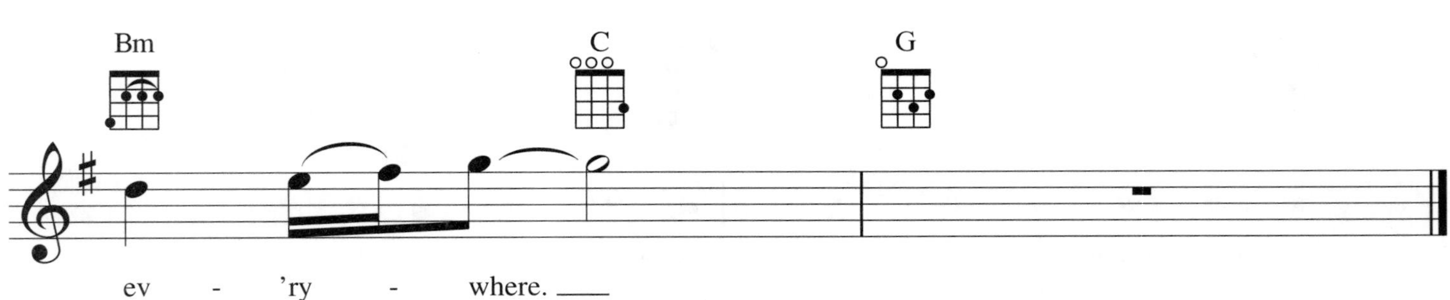
Bm
C
G
ev - 'ry - where.

Hey Jude

Words and Music by John Lennon and Paul McCartney

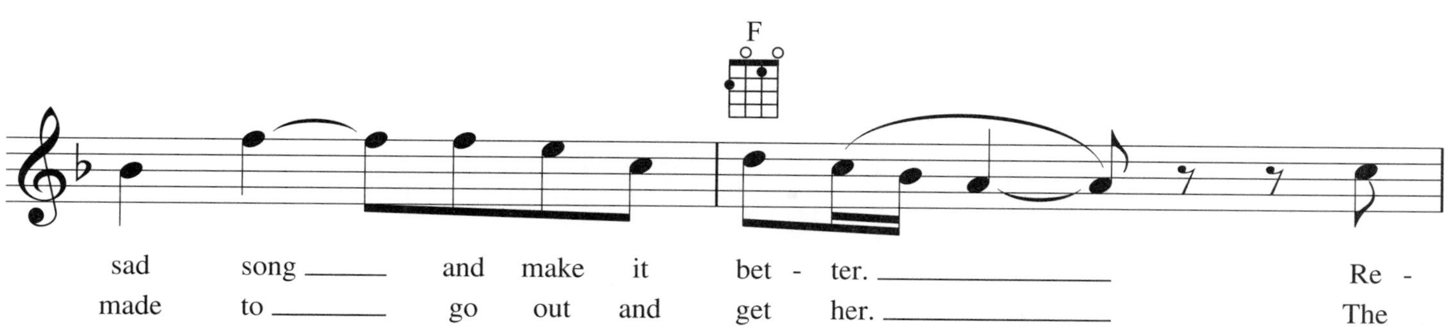

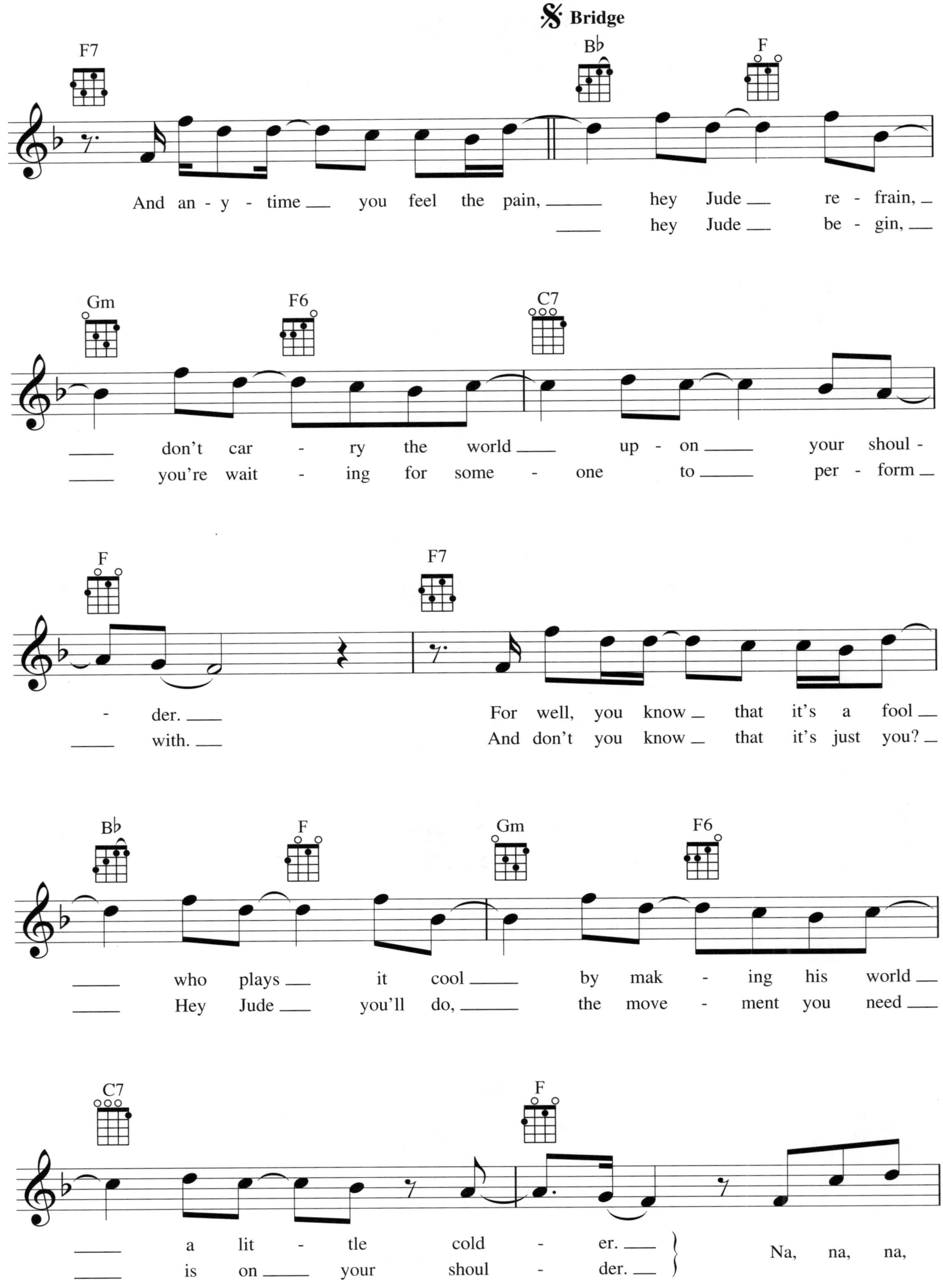

Bridge

F7 Bb F

And an - y - time you feel the pain, hey Jude re - frain,
hey Jude be - gin,

Gm F6 C7

don't car - ry the world up - on your shoul -
you're wait - ing for some - one to per - form

F F7

- der. For well, you know that it's a fool
with. And don't you know that it's just you?

Bb F Gm F6

who plays it cool by mak - ing his world
Hey Jude you'll do, the move - ment you need

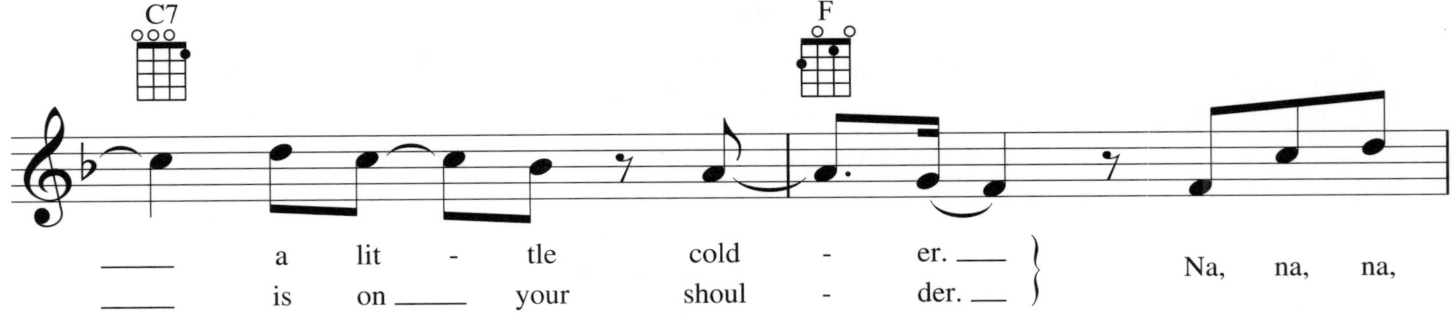

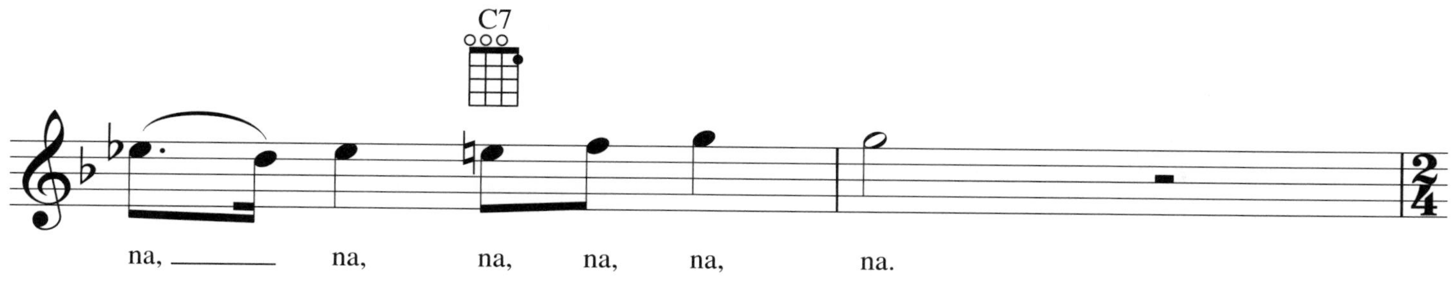
C7
na, na, na, na, na, na.

To Coda
Verse
F
C7
3., 4. Hey Jude don't let me down. You have

F
B♭
found her, now go and get her. Re - mem - ber to let her in - to your

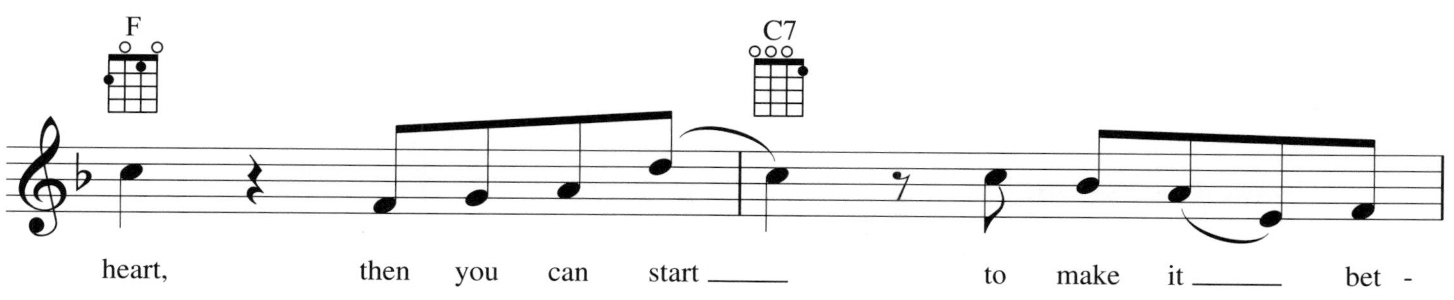
F
C7
heart, then you can start to make it bet -

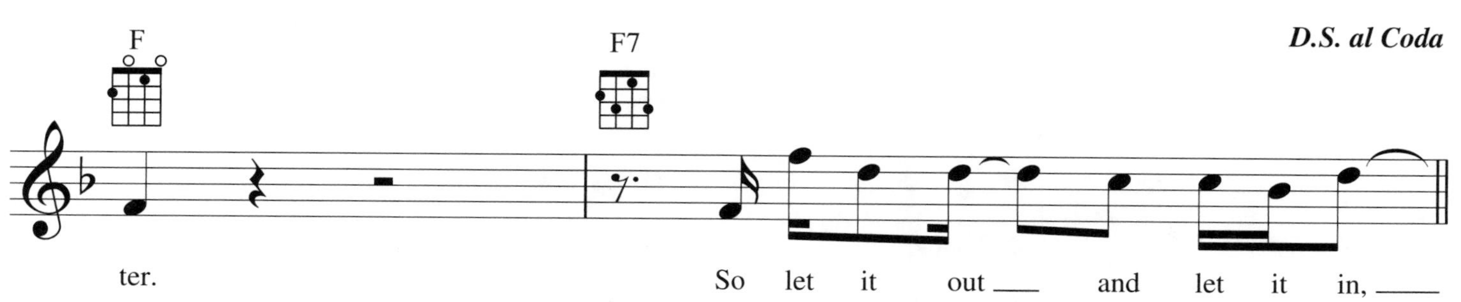
F
F7
D.S. al Coda
ter. So let it out and let it in,

Coda
Verse
F
C7
3
Jude ___ don't make it bad, take a

F
B♭
sad song and make it bet - ter. ___ Re - mem - ber to let her un - der your

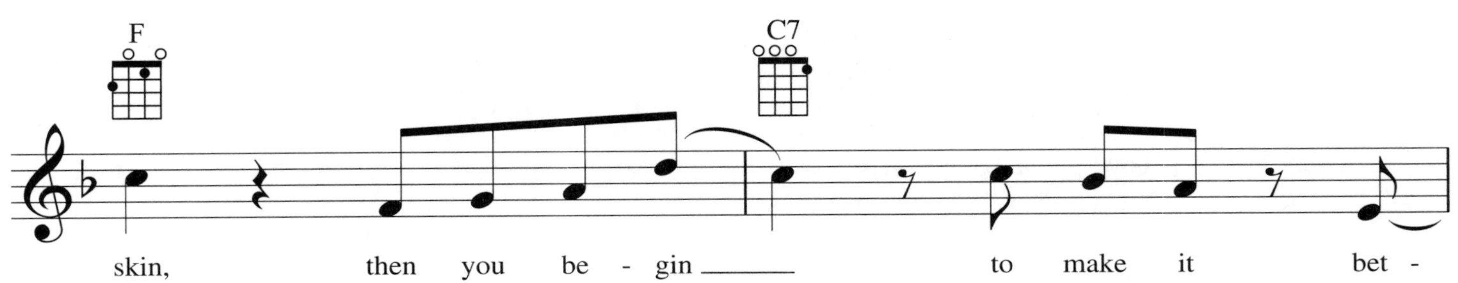
F
C7
skin, then you be - gin ___ to make it bet -

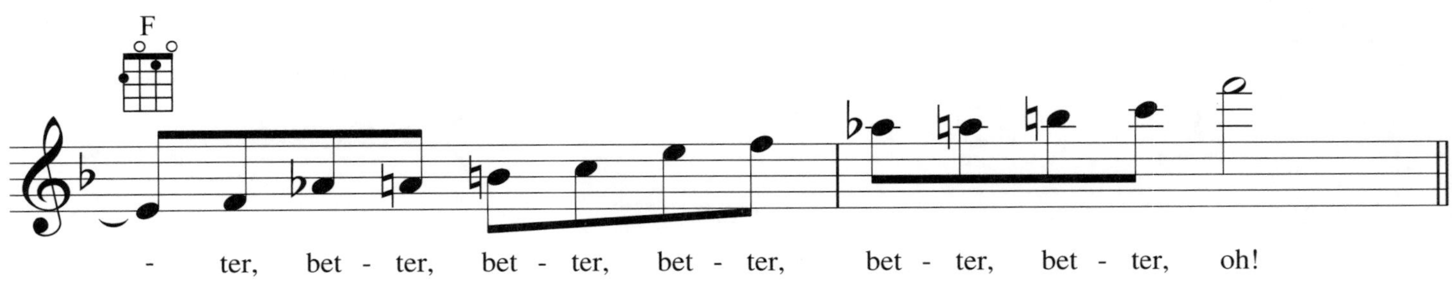
F
- ter, bet - ter, bet - ter, bet - ter, bet - ter, bet - ter, oh!

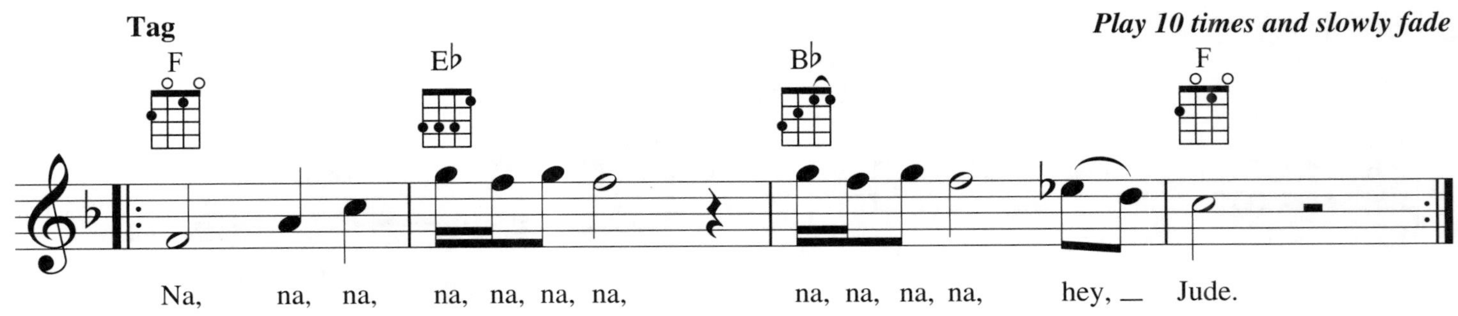
Tag
Play 10 times and slowly fade
F
E♭
B♭
F
Na, na, na, na, na, na, na, na, na, na, na, hey, _ Jude.

I Want to Hold Your Hand

Words and Music by John Lennon and Paul McCartney

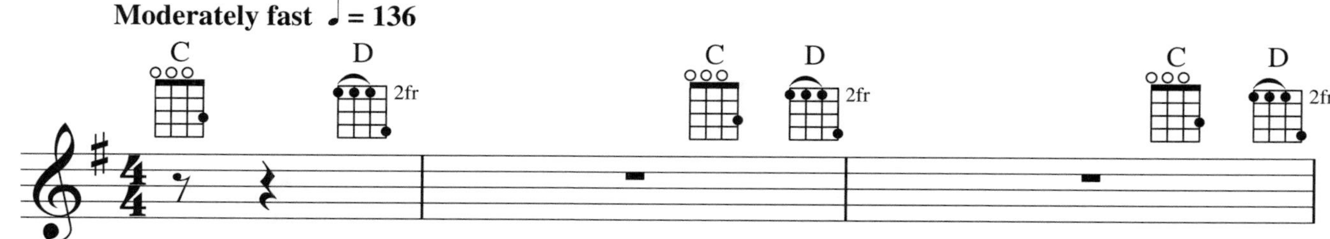

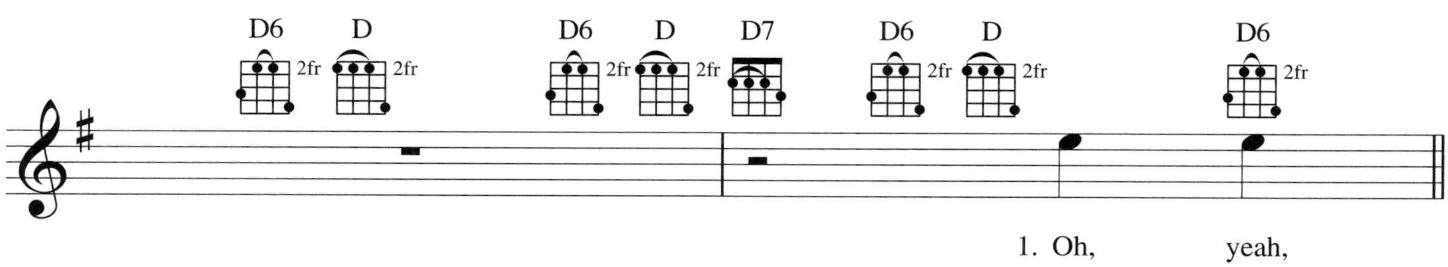

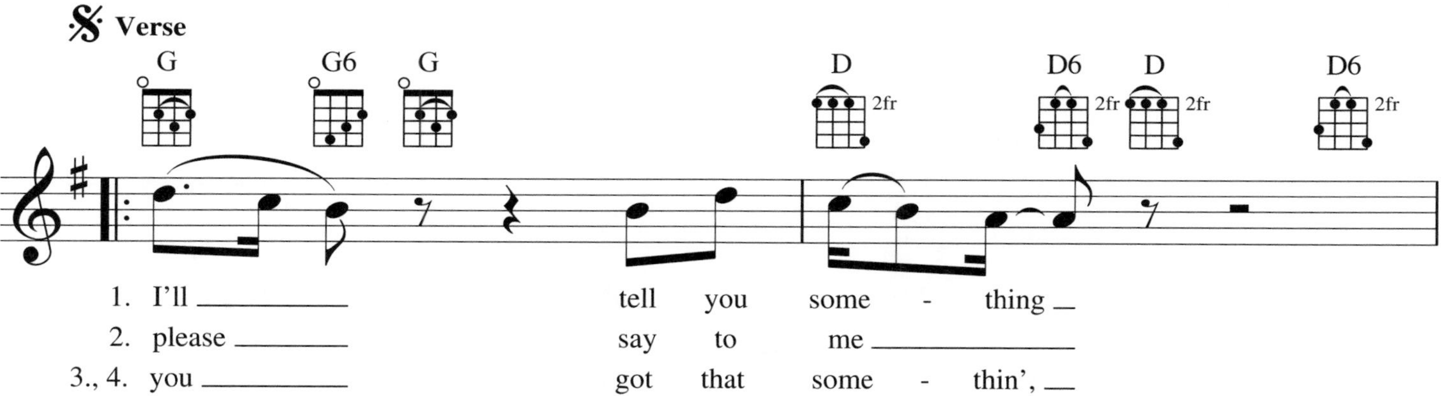

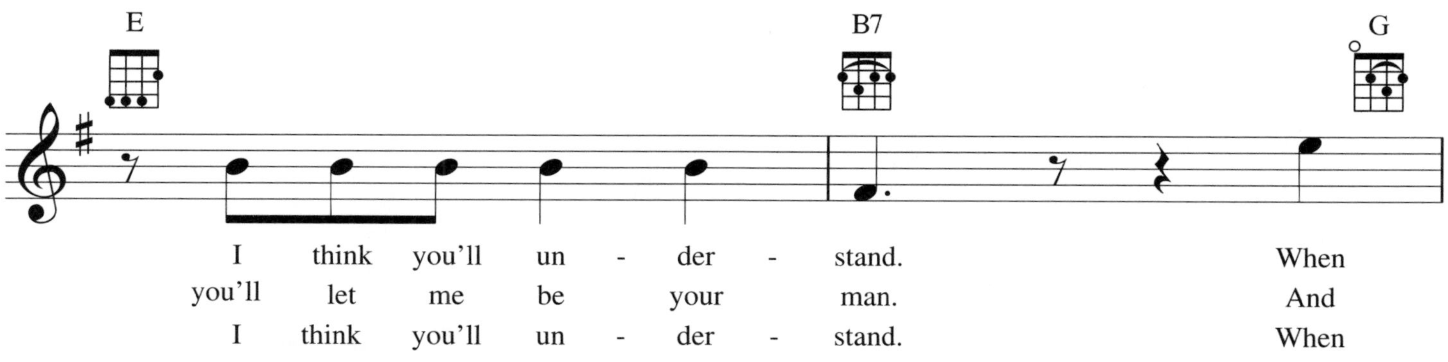

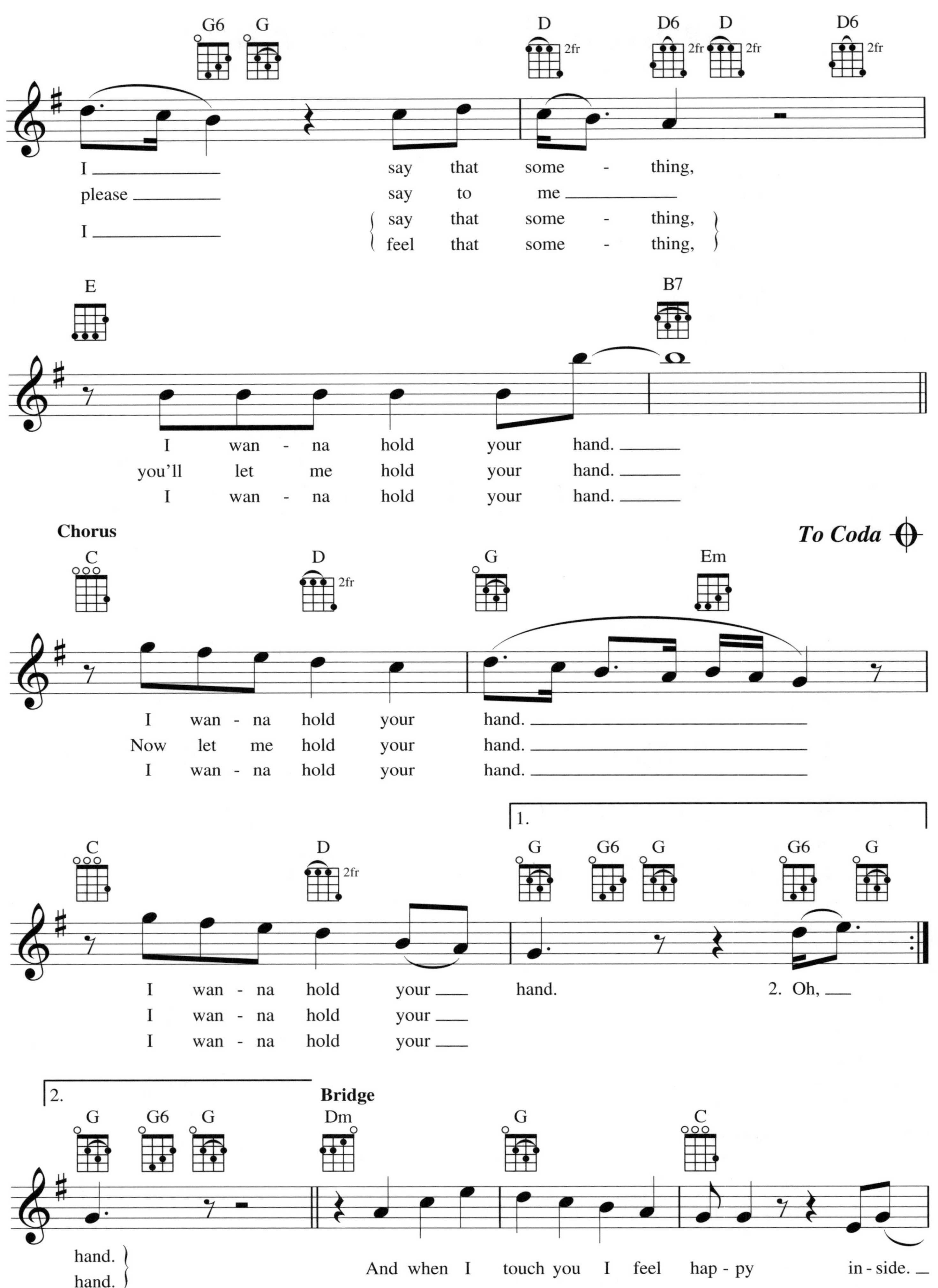
G6 G D D6 D D6
2fr
I say that some - thing,
please say to me
I say that some - thing,
feel that some - thing,
E B7
I wan - na hold your hand.
you'll let me hold your hand.
I wan - na hold your hand.
Chorus
To Coda
C D G Em
I wan - na hold your hand.
Now let me hold your hand.
I wan - na hold your hand.
1.
C D G G6 G G6 G
I wan - na hold your hand. 2. Oh,
I wan - na hold your
I wan - na hold your
2.
Bridge
G G6 G Dm G C
hand.
hand.
And when I touch you I feel hap - py in - side.

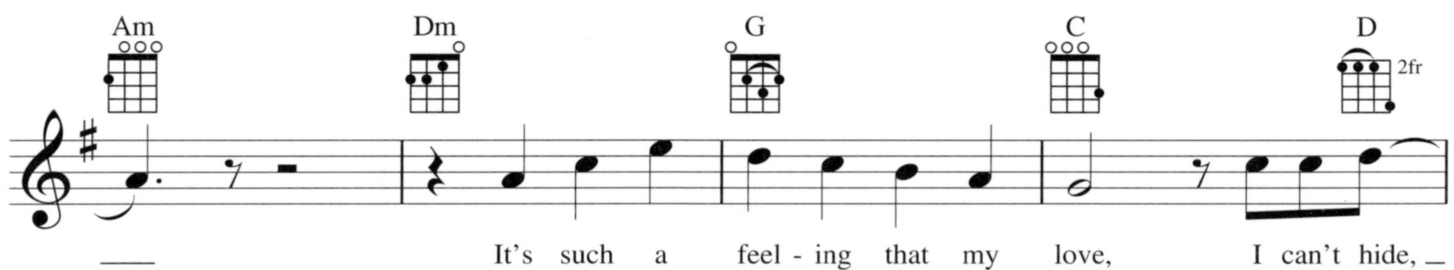
Am
Dm
G
C
D
2fr
It's such a feel - ing that my love, I can't hide,

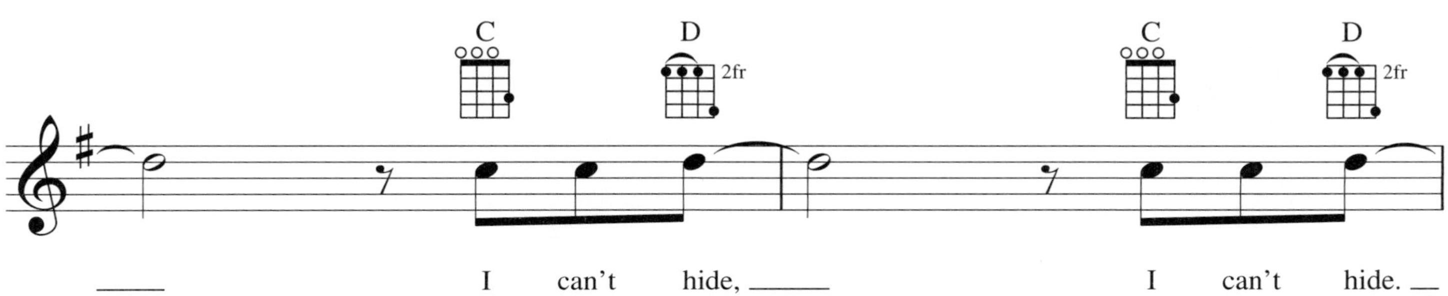
C
D
2fr
C
D
2fr
I can't hide,
I can't hide.

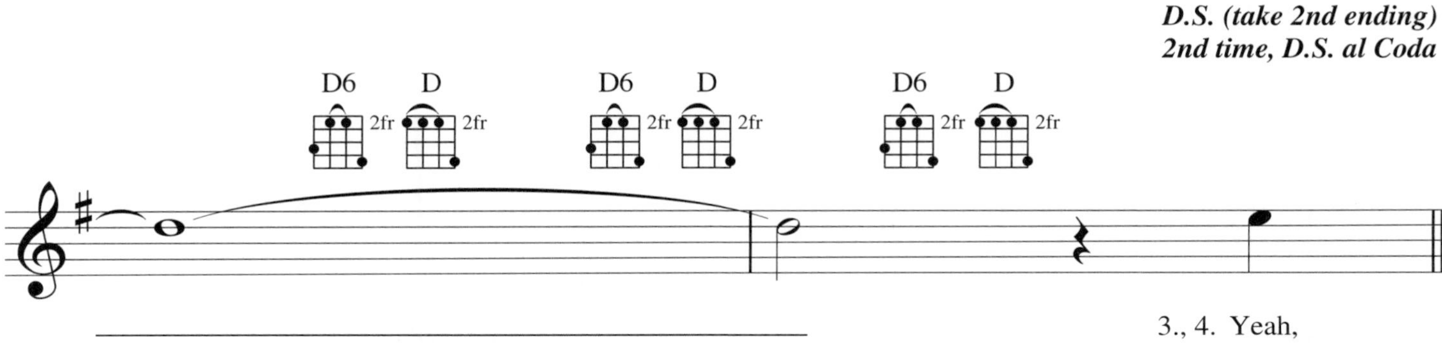
D.S. (take 2nd ending)
2nd time, D.S. al Coda
D6
D
2fr
D6
D
2fr
D6
D
2fr
3., 4. Yeah,

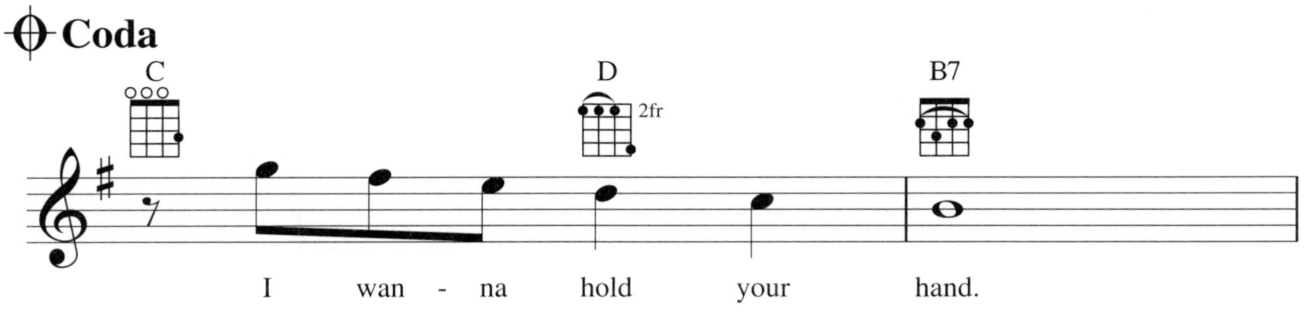
Coda
C
D
2fr
B7
I wan - na hold your hand.

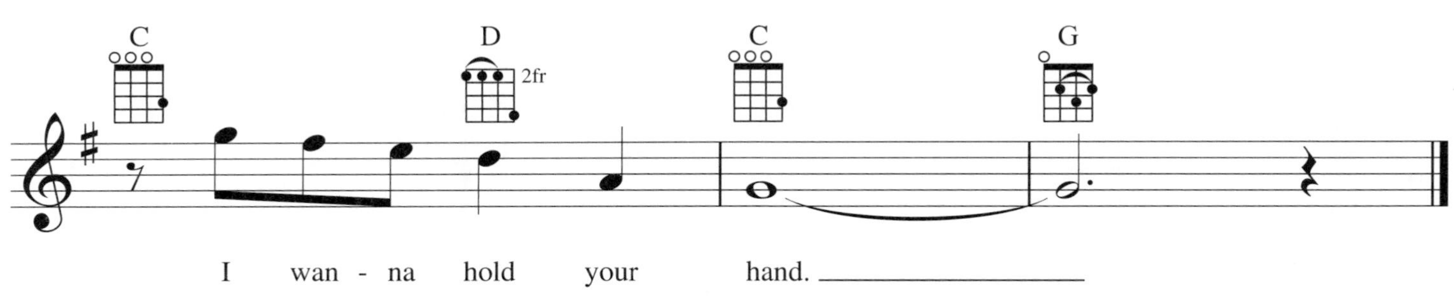
C
D
2fr
C
G
I wan - na hold your hand.

Let It Be

Words and Music by John Lennon and Paul McCartney

Chorus
F
C
Am
G6
be. ___ Let it be, ___ let it be. Ah, let it be, ___

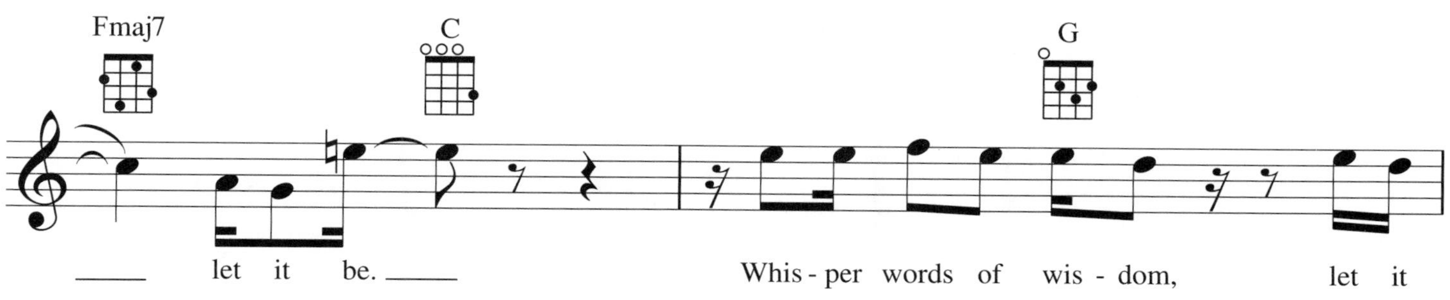
Fmaj7
C
G
___ let it be. ___ Whis - per words of wis - dom, let it

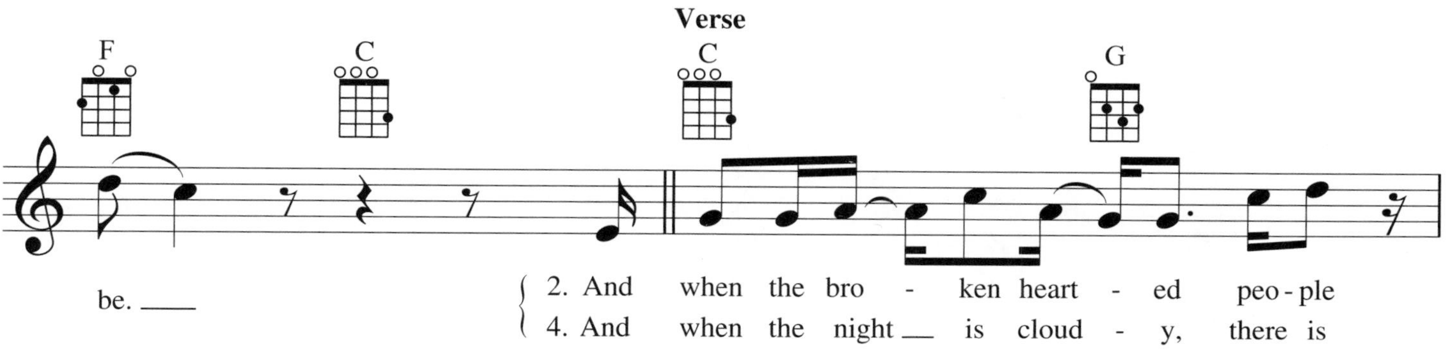
Verse
F
C
C
G
be. ___
2. And when the bro - ken heart - ed peo - ple
4. And when the night ___ is cloud - y, there is

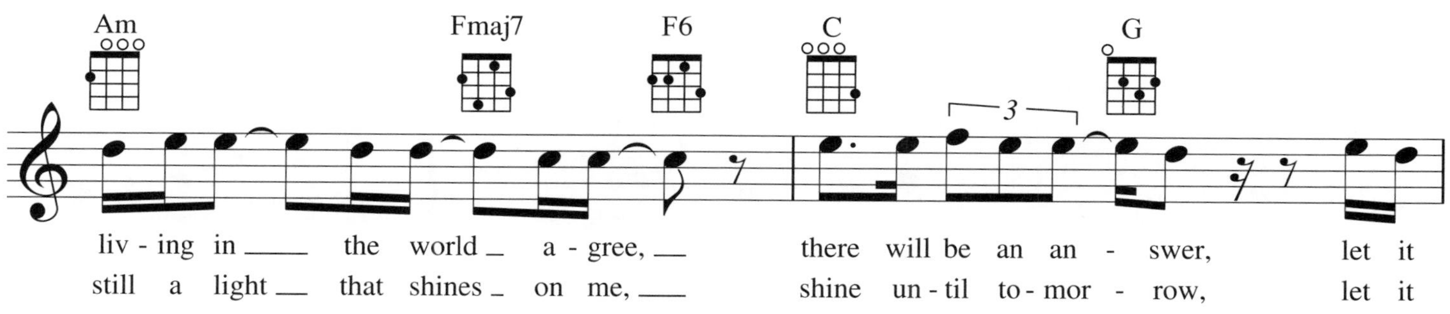
Am
Fmaj7
F6
C
G
3
liv - ing in ___ the world ___ a - gree, ___ there will be an an - swer, let it
still a light ___ that shines ___ on me, ___ shine un - til to - mor - row, let it

F
C
G
be. ___ For though they may ___ be part - ed, there is
be. ___ I wake up to ___ the sound ___ of mu - sic,

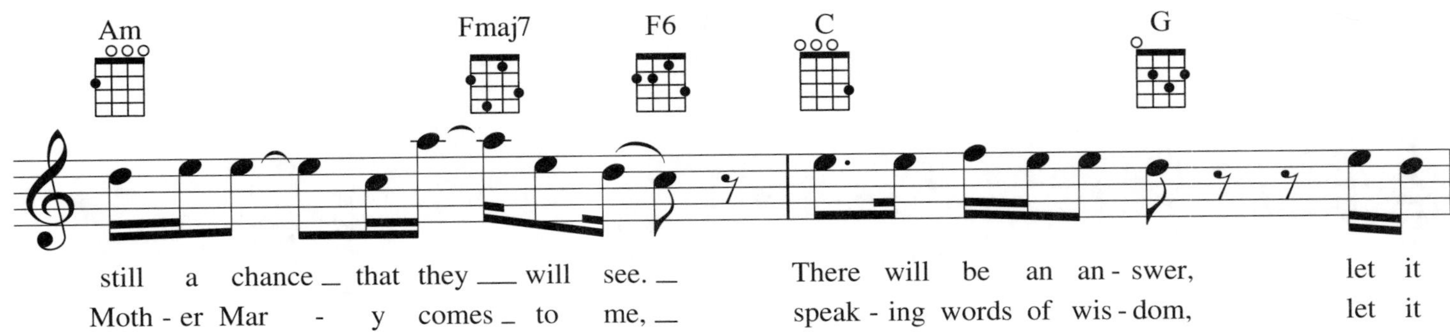
Am
Fmaj7
F6
C
G
still a chance _ that they _ will see. _
Moth - er Mar - y comes _ to me, _
There will be an an - swer, let it
speak - ing words of wis - dom, let it

Chorus
F
C
Am
G6
be. _
be. _
Let it be, _ let it be. _ Ah, let it be, _

To Coda
Fmaj7
C
G
_ let it be. _ Yeah, there will be an an - swer, let it

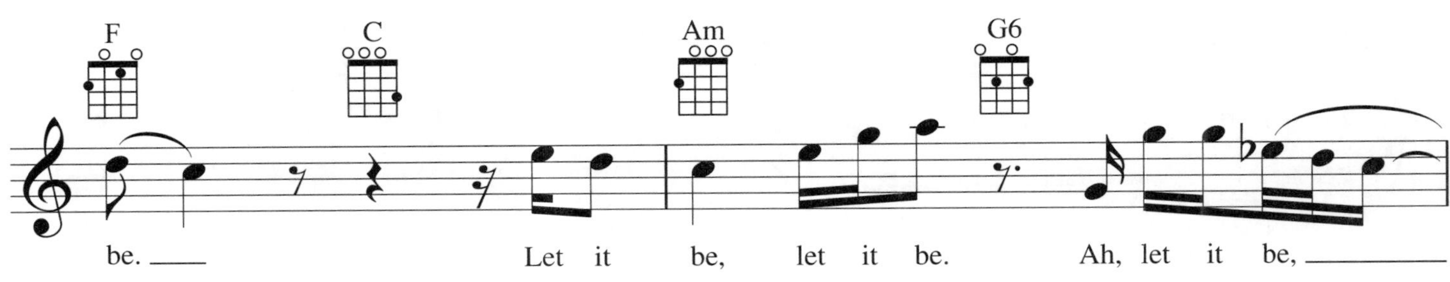
F
C
Am
G6
be. _ Let it be, let it be. Ah, let it be, _

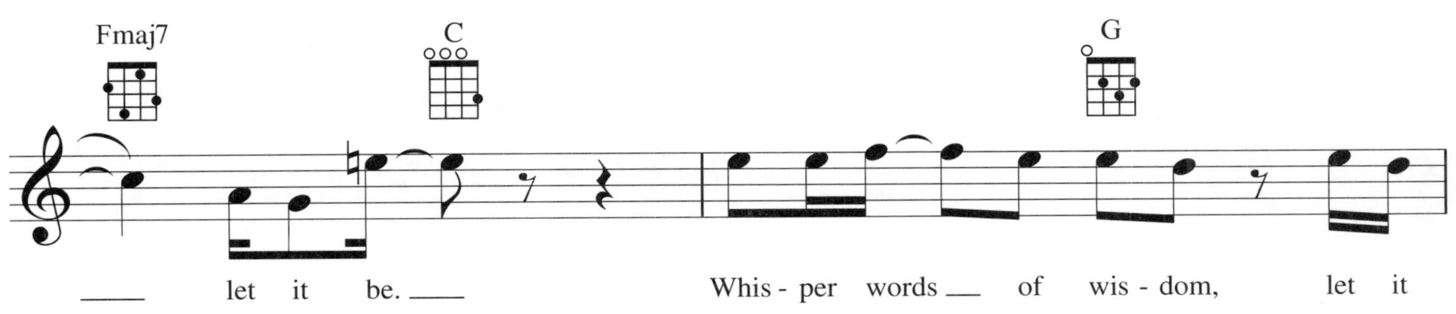
Fmaj7
C
G
_ let it be. _ Whis - per words _ of wis - dom, let it

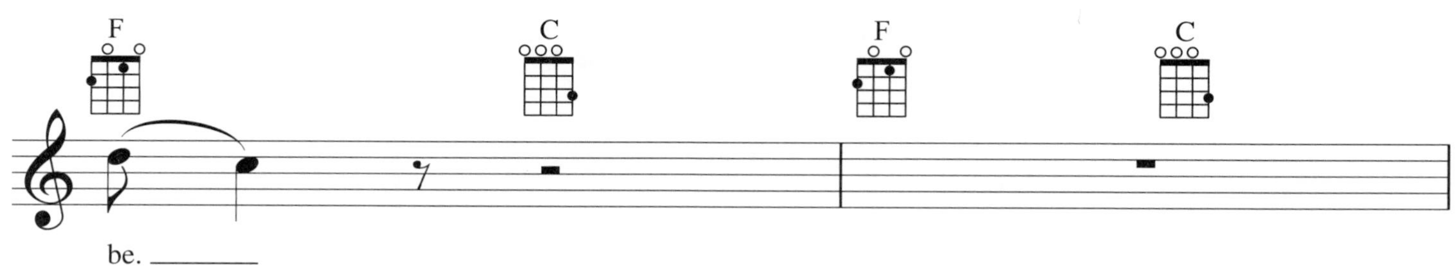
F
C
F
C
be.

D.S. al Coda

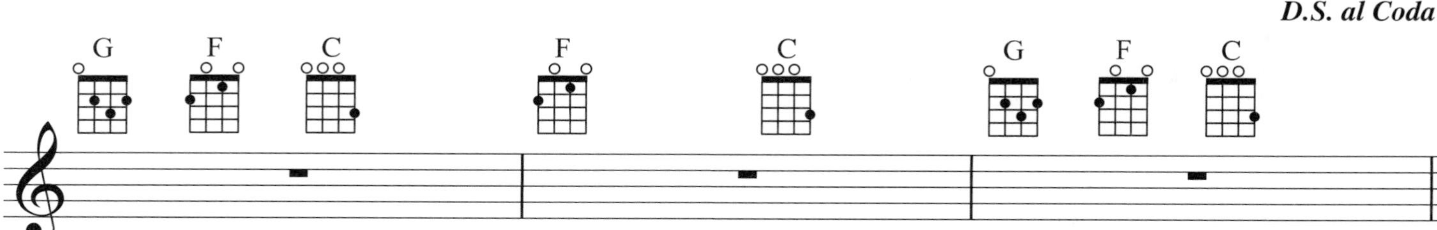
G
F
C
F
C
G
F
C

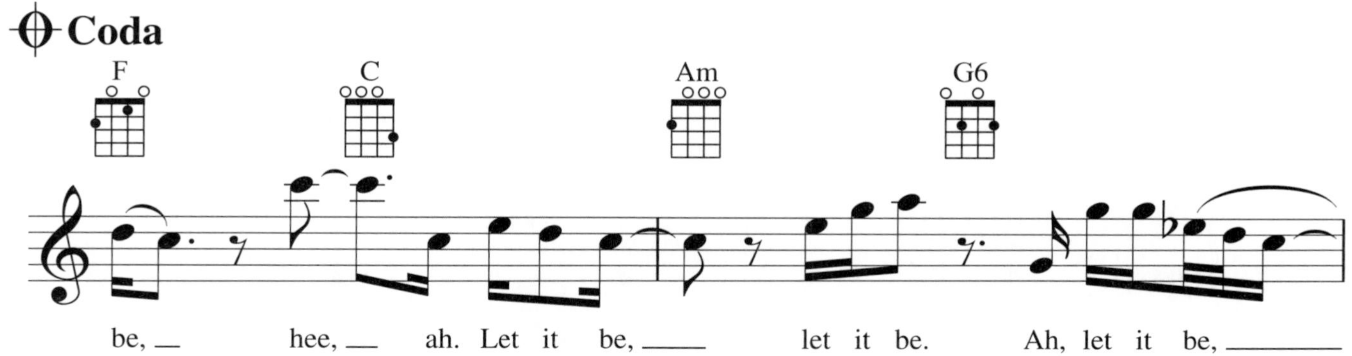
Coda
F
C
Am
G6
be, hee, ah. Let it be, let it be. Ah, let it be,

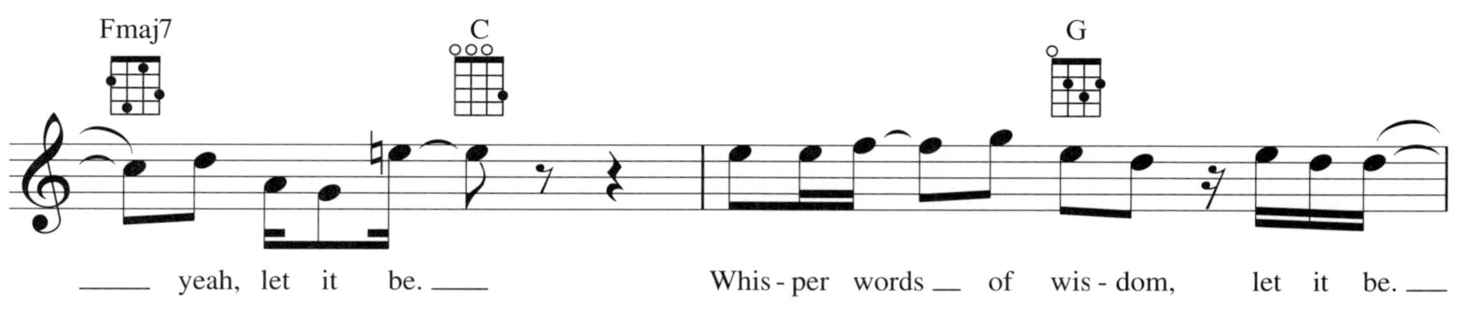
Fmaj7
C
G
yeah, let it be. Whis - per words of wis - dom, let it be.

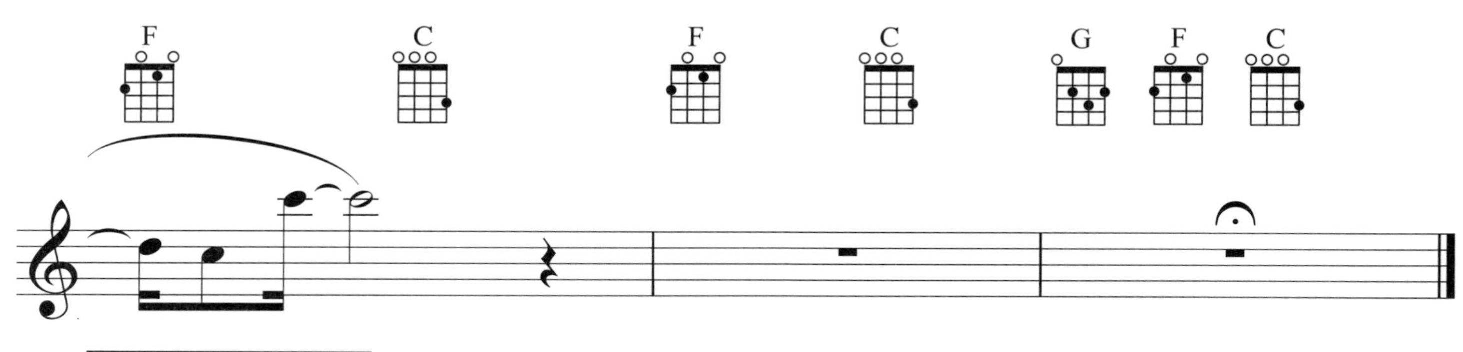
F
C
F
C
G
F
C

Love Me Do

Words and Music by John Lennon and Paul McCartney

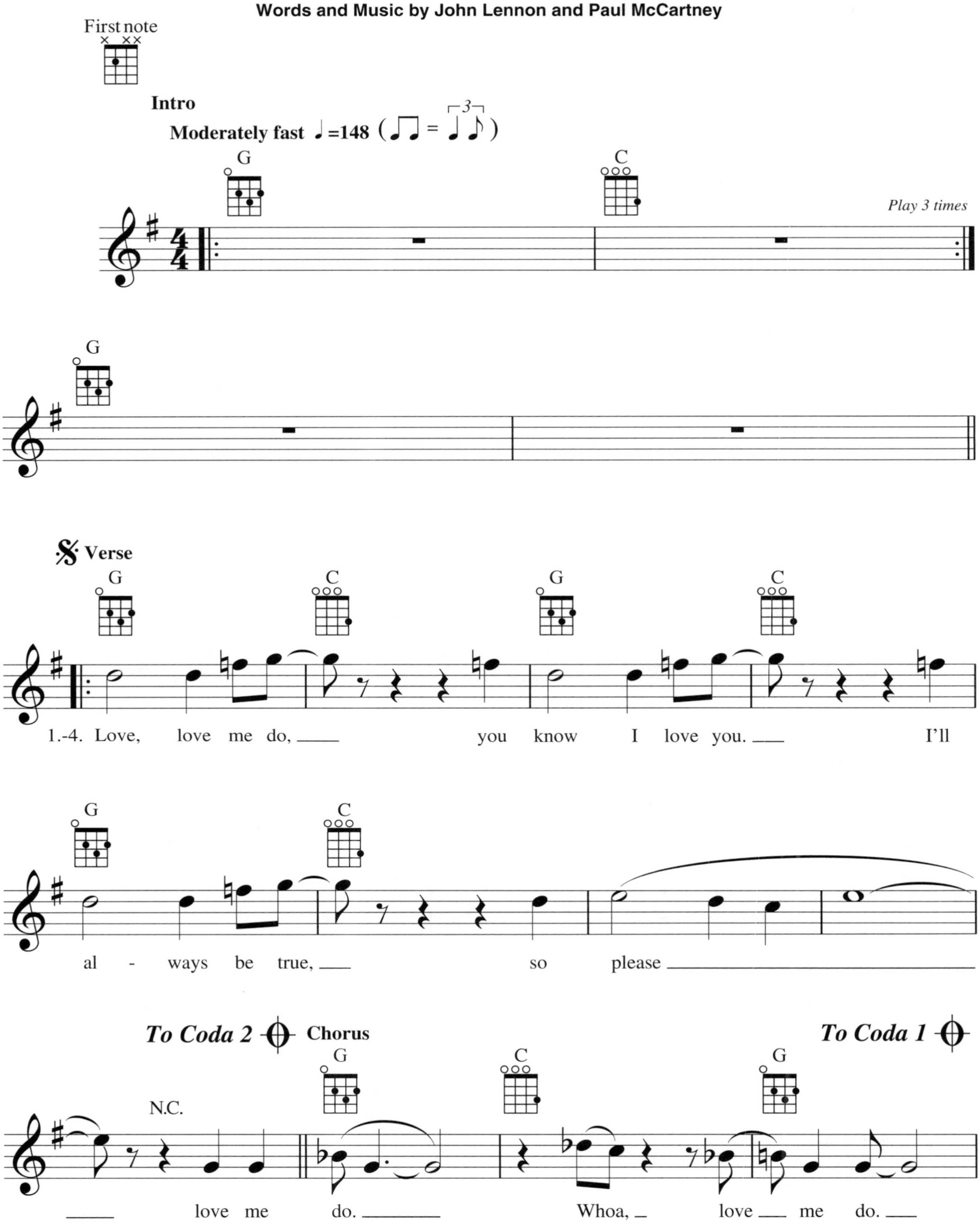

First note

Intro

Moderately fast ♩ = 148 (♫ = ♩ ♪ triplet)

G C

Play 3 times

G

Verse

G C G C

1.-4. Love, love me do, you know I love you. I'll

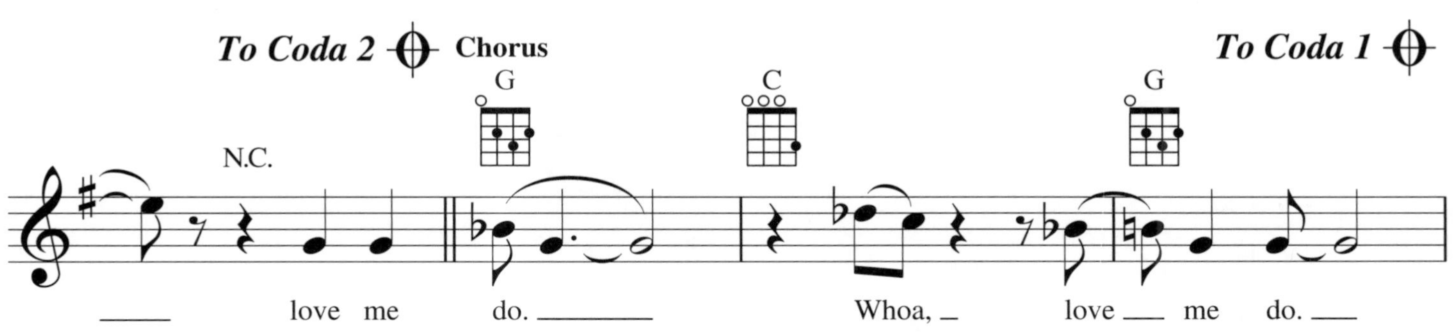

Bridge
C
D
C
Some - one to love, some - bod - y

D.S. al Coda 1
G
D
C
G
new. Some - one to love, some - one like you.

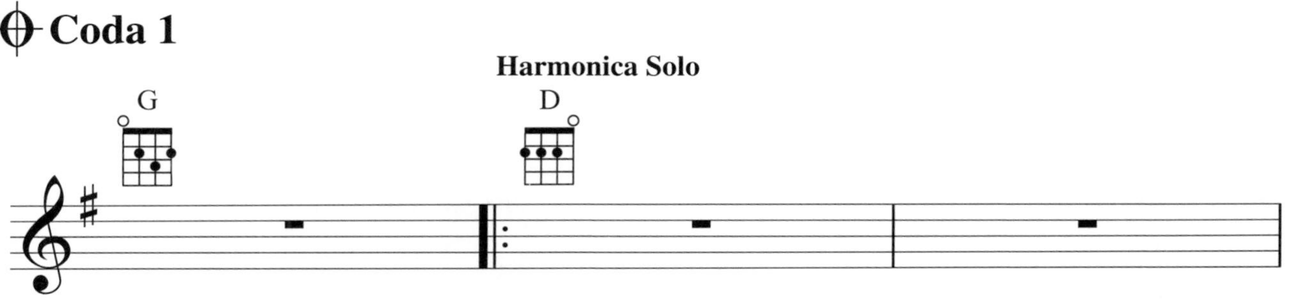
Coda 1
Harmonica Solo
G
D

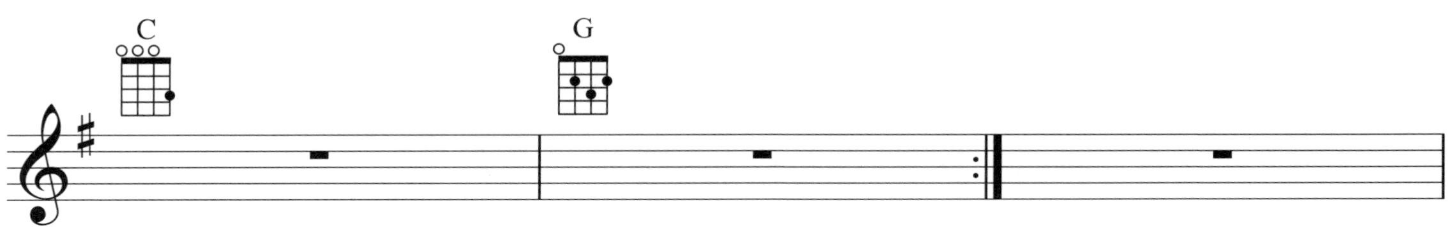
C
G

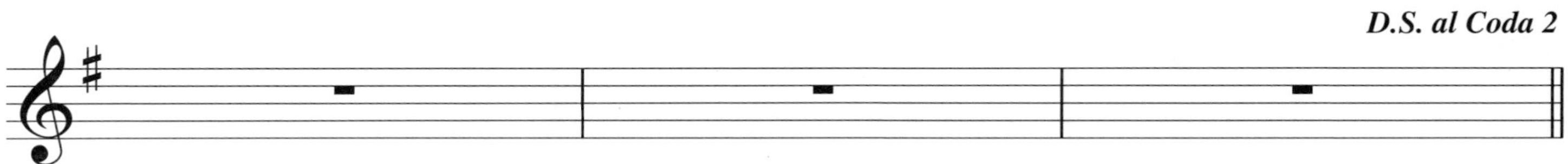
D.S. al Coda 2

Coda 2

Chorus

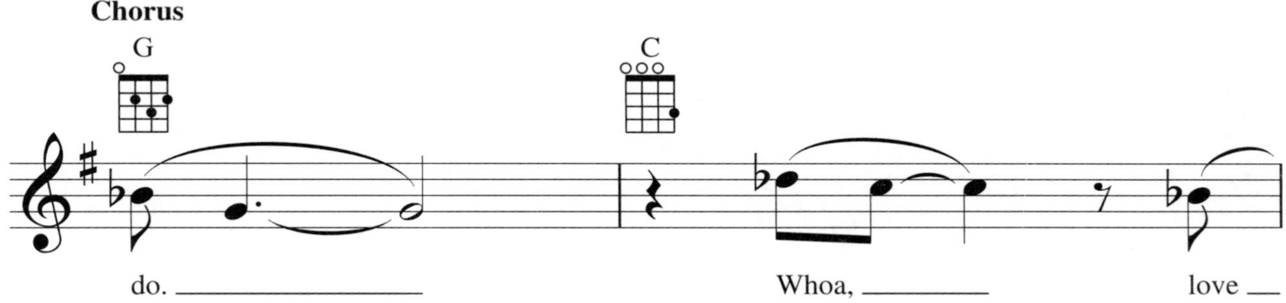

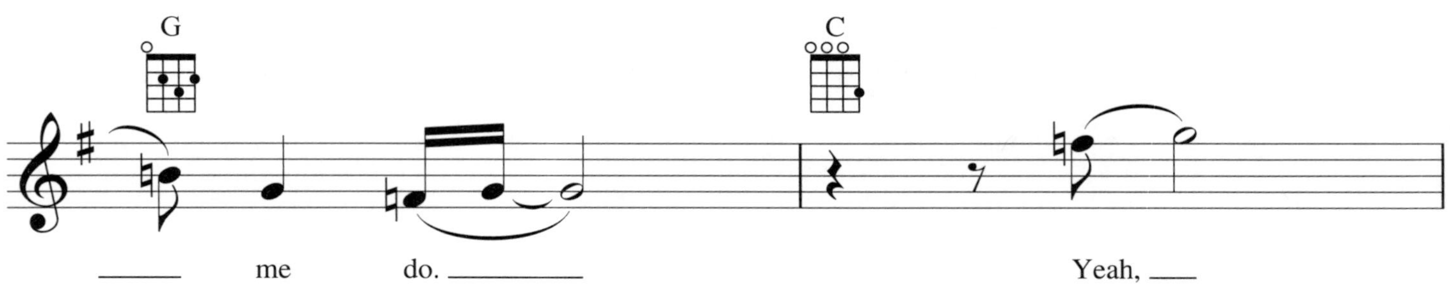

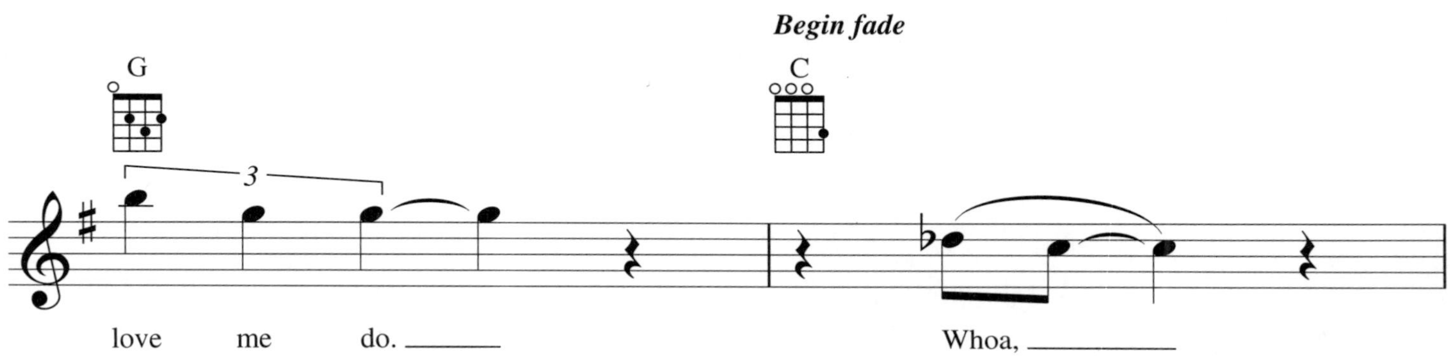

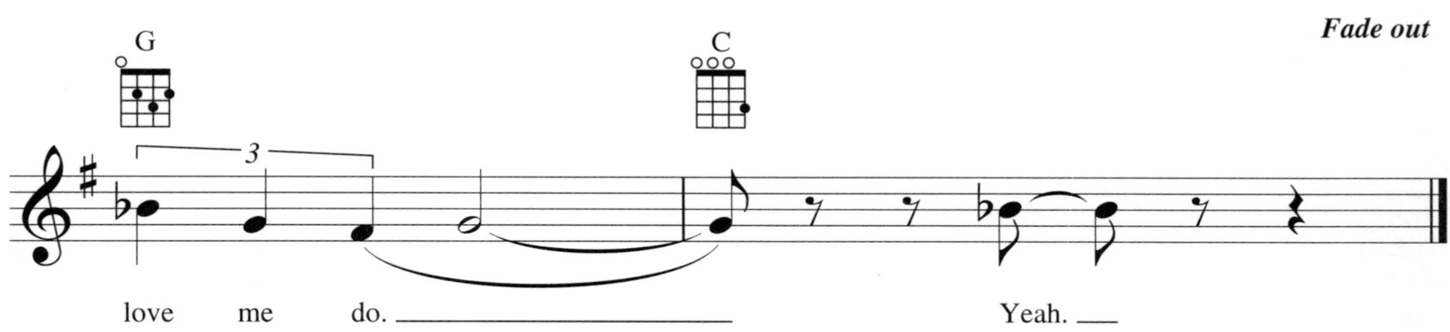

Michelle

Words and Music by John Lennon and Paul McCartney

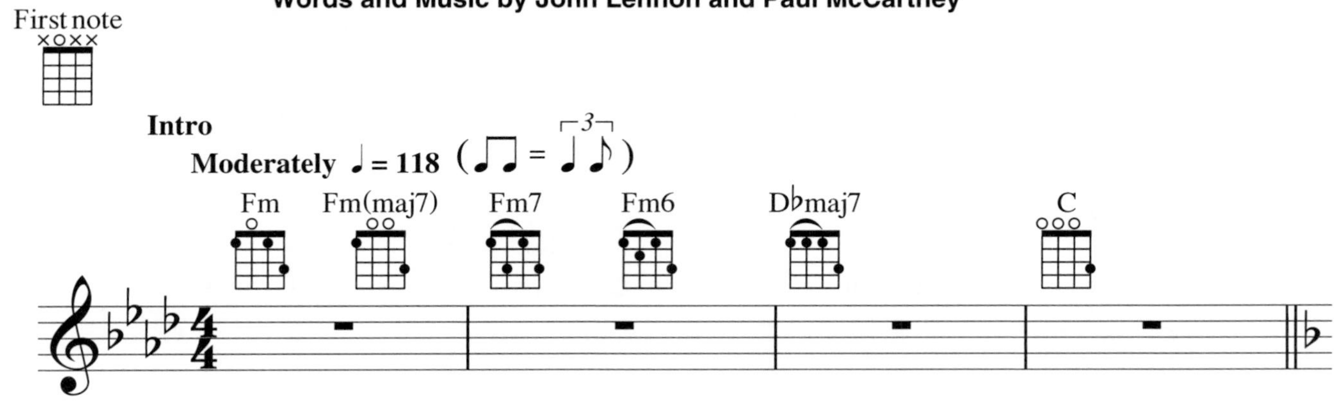

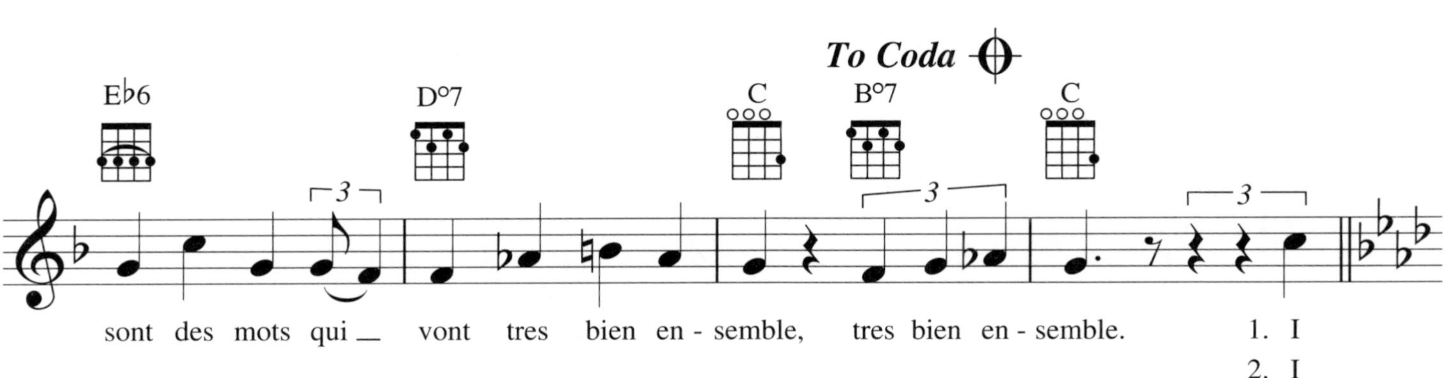

Verse
Fm
A♭7
love you, I love you, I love you, that's all I want to
need to, I need to, I need to, I need to make you
want you, I want you, I want you, I think you know by

D♭
C7
Fm
say, un - til I find a way. I will
see, oh, what you mean to me. Un -
now, I'll get to you some - how. Un -

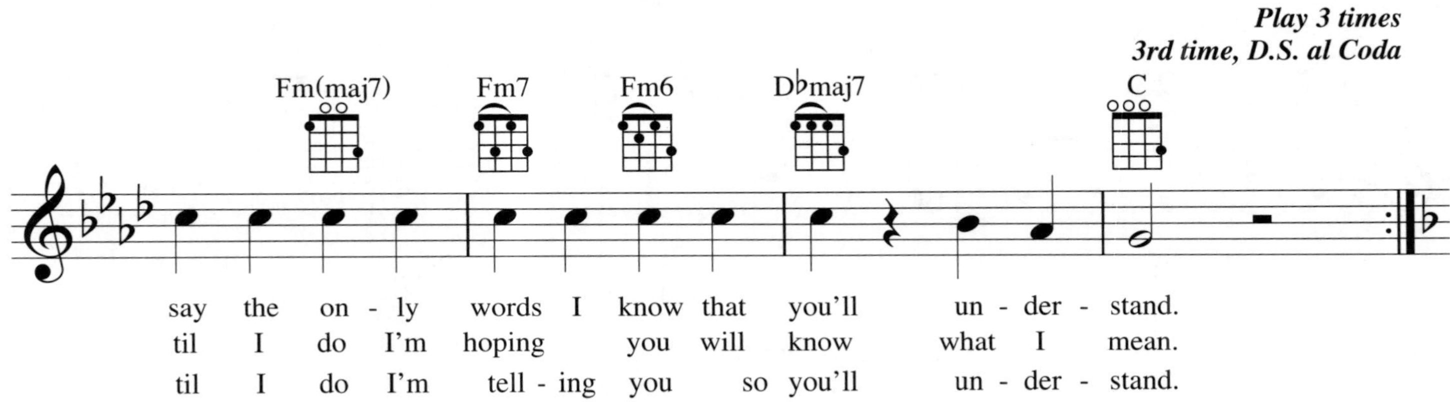
Play 3 times
3rd time, D.S. al Coda
Fm(maj7)
Fm7
Fm6
D♭maj7
C
say the on - ly words I know that you'll un - der - stand.
til I do I'm hoping you will know what I mean.
til I do I'm tell - ing you so you'll un - der - stand.

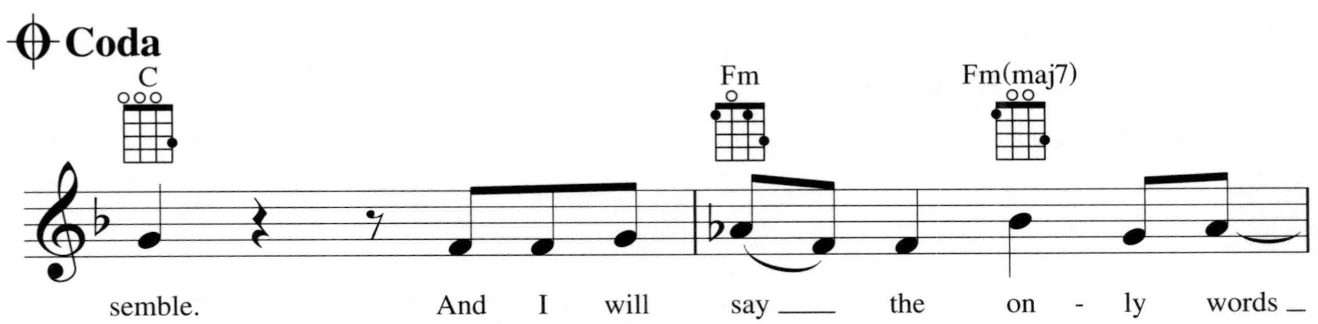
Coda
C
Fm
Fm(maj7)
semble. And I will say the on - ly words

Fm7
Fm6
D♭maj7
C
3
I know that you'll un - der - stand, my Mi -

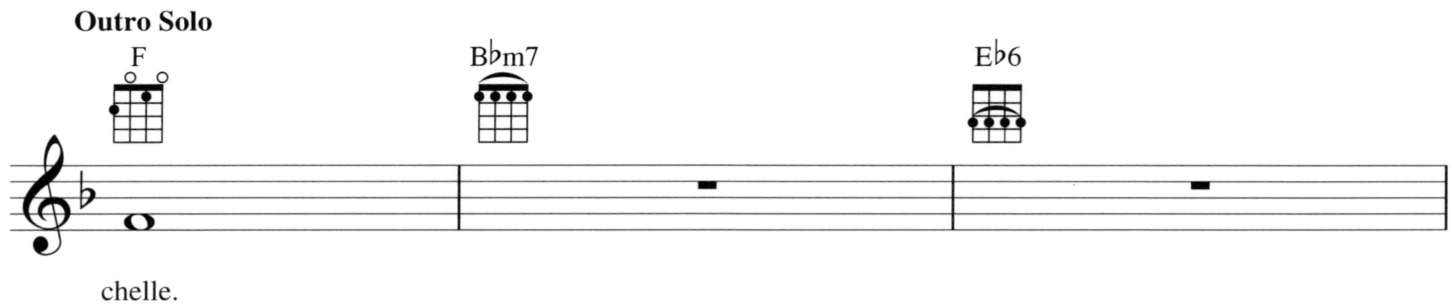
Outro Solo
F
B♭m7
E♭6
chelle.

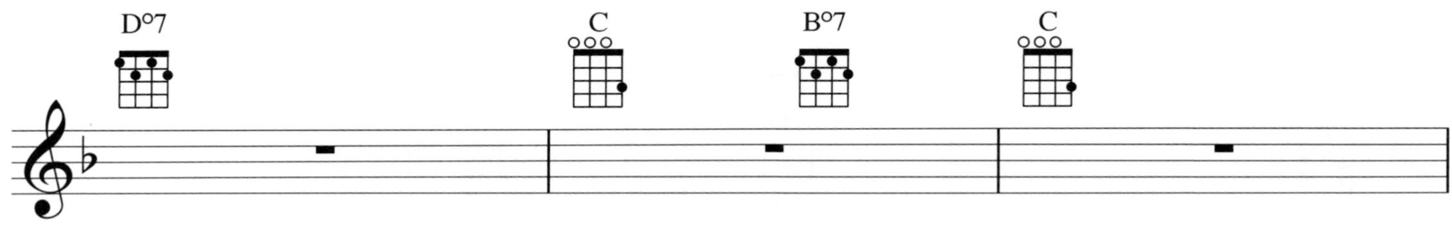
D°7
C
B°7
C

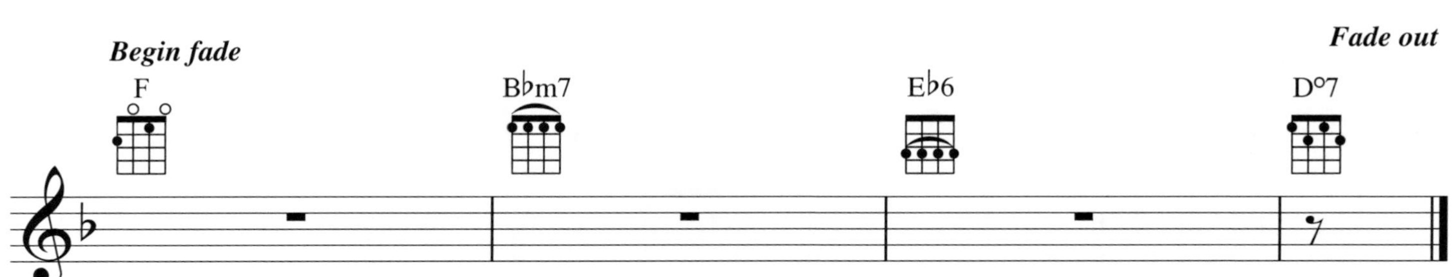
Begin fade
Fade out
F
B♭m7
E♭6
D°7

Nowhere Man

Words and Music by John Lennon and Paul McCartney

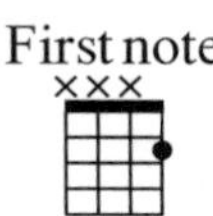

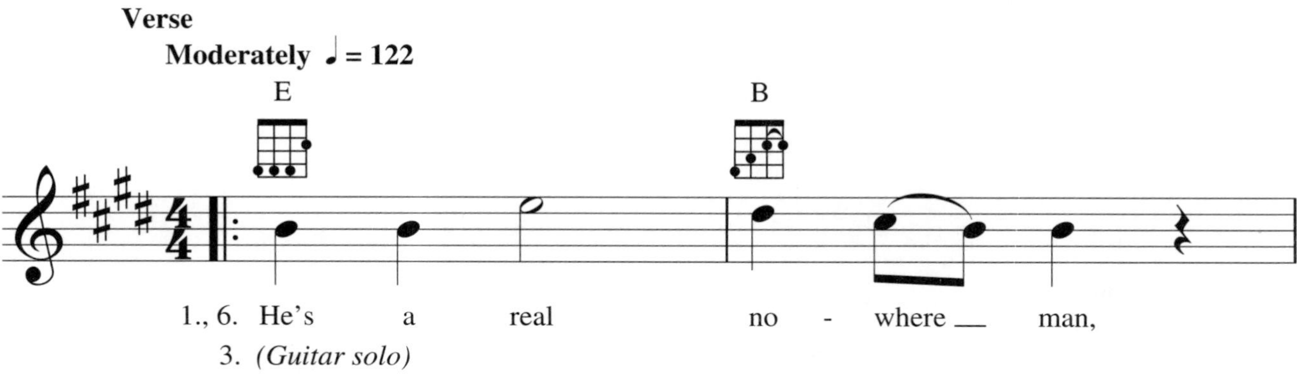

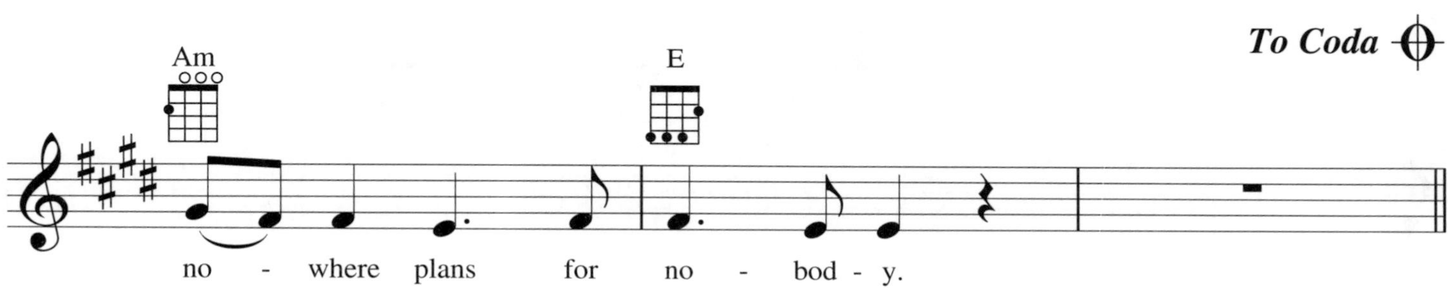

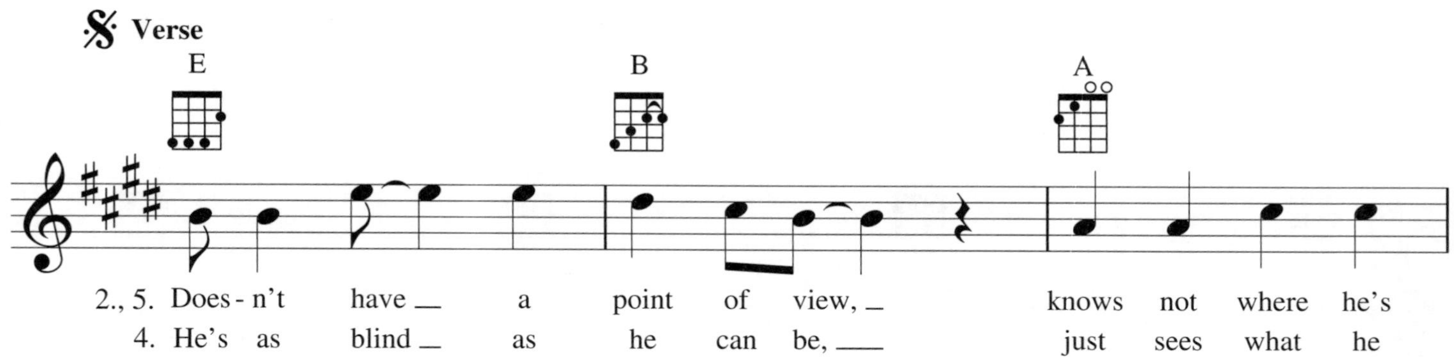

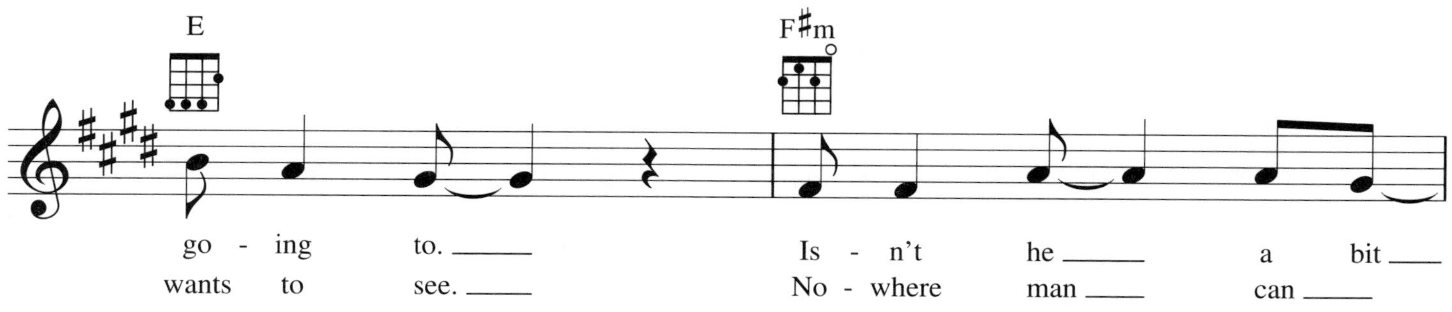
E
F♯m
go - ing to.
wants to see.
Is - n't he a bit
No - where man can

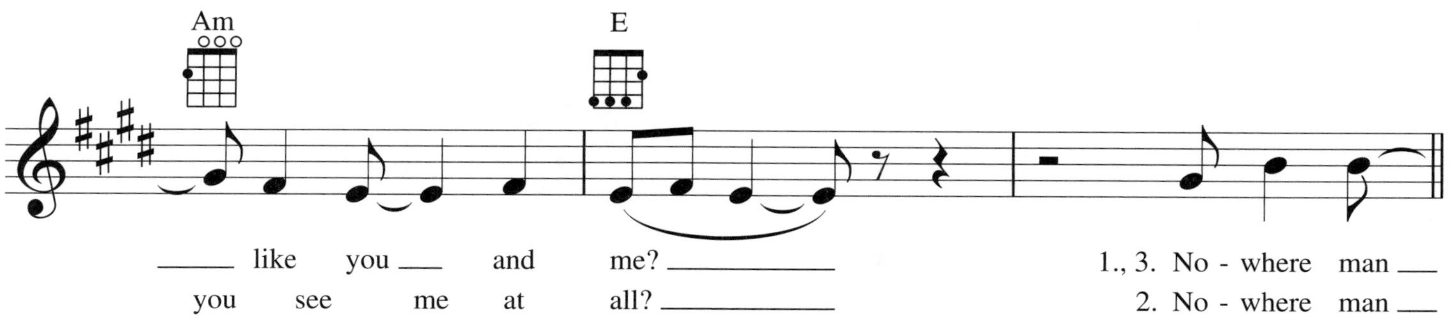
Am
E
like you and me?
you see me at all?
1., 3. No - where man
2. No - where man

Chorus

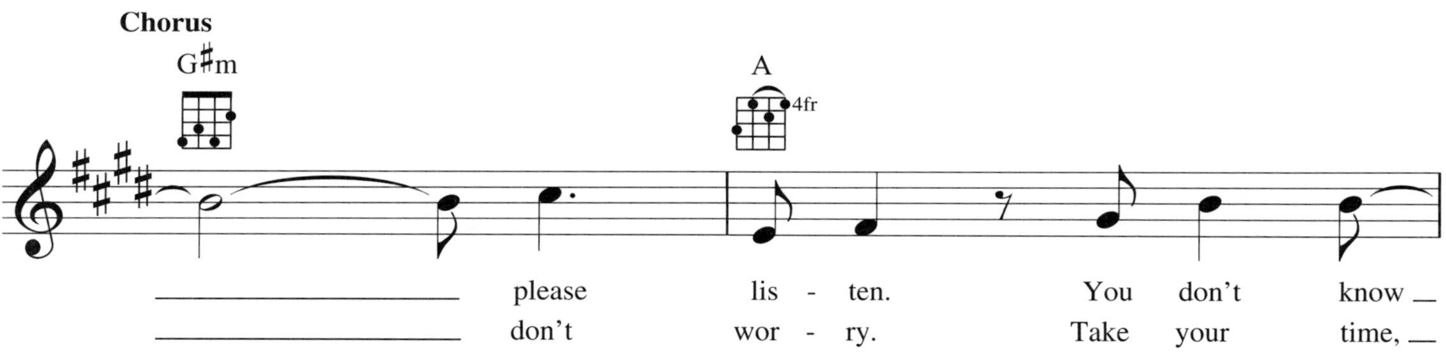
G♯m
A
4fr
please lis - ten. You don't know
don't wor - ry. Take your time,

G♯m
A
4fr
G♯m
what you're miss - ing. No - where man, the
don't hur - ry. Leave it all 'til

2nd time, D.S.
3rd time, D.C. al Coda

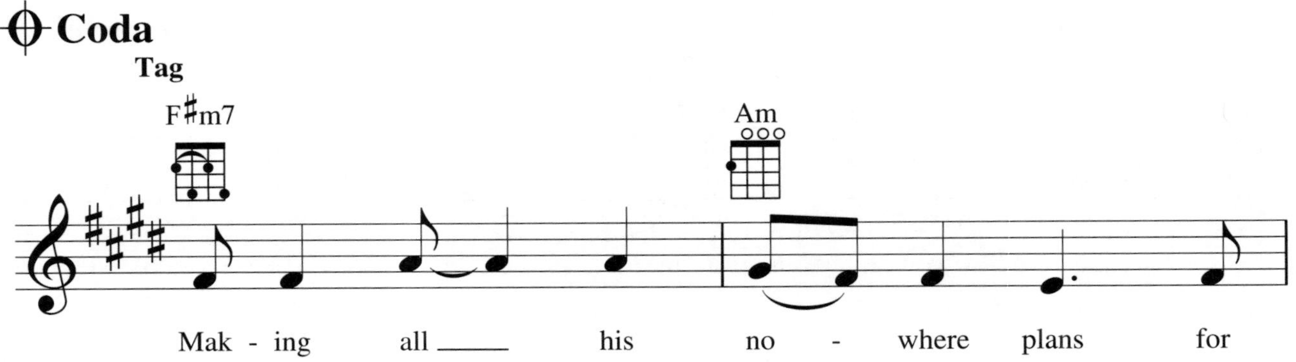

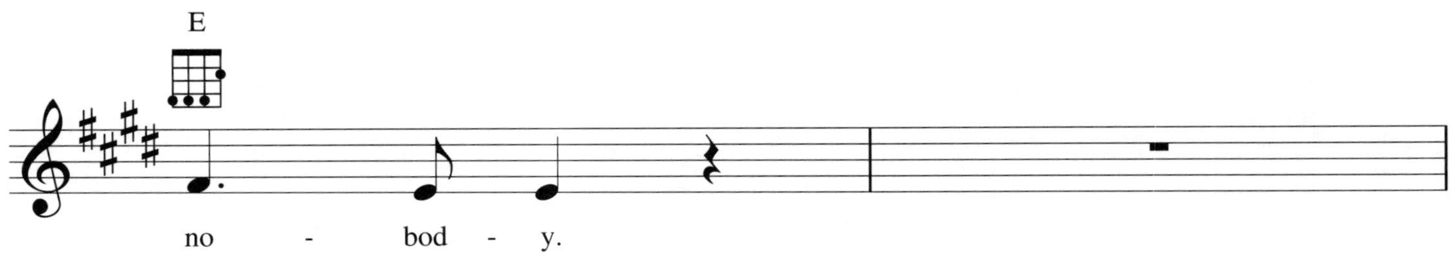

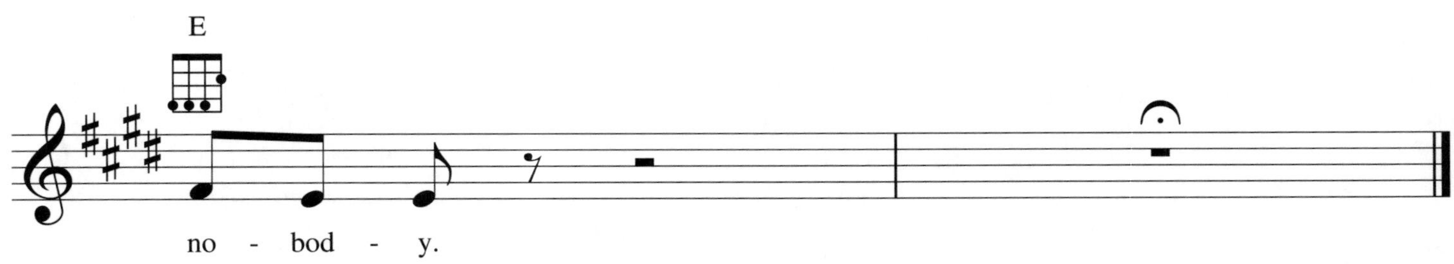

Ob-La-Di, Ob-La-Da

Words and Music by John Lennon and Paul McCartney

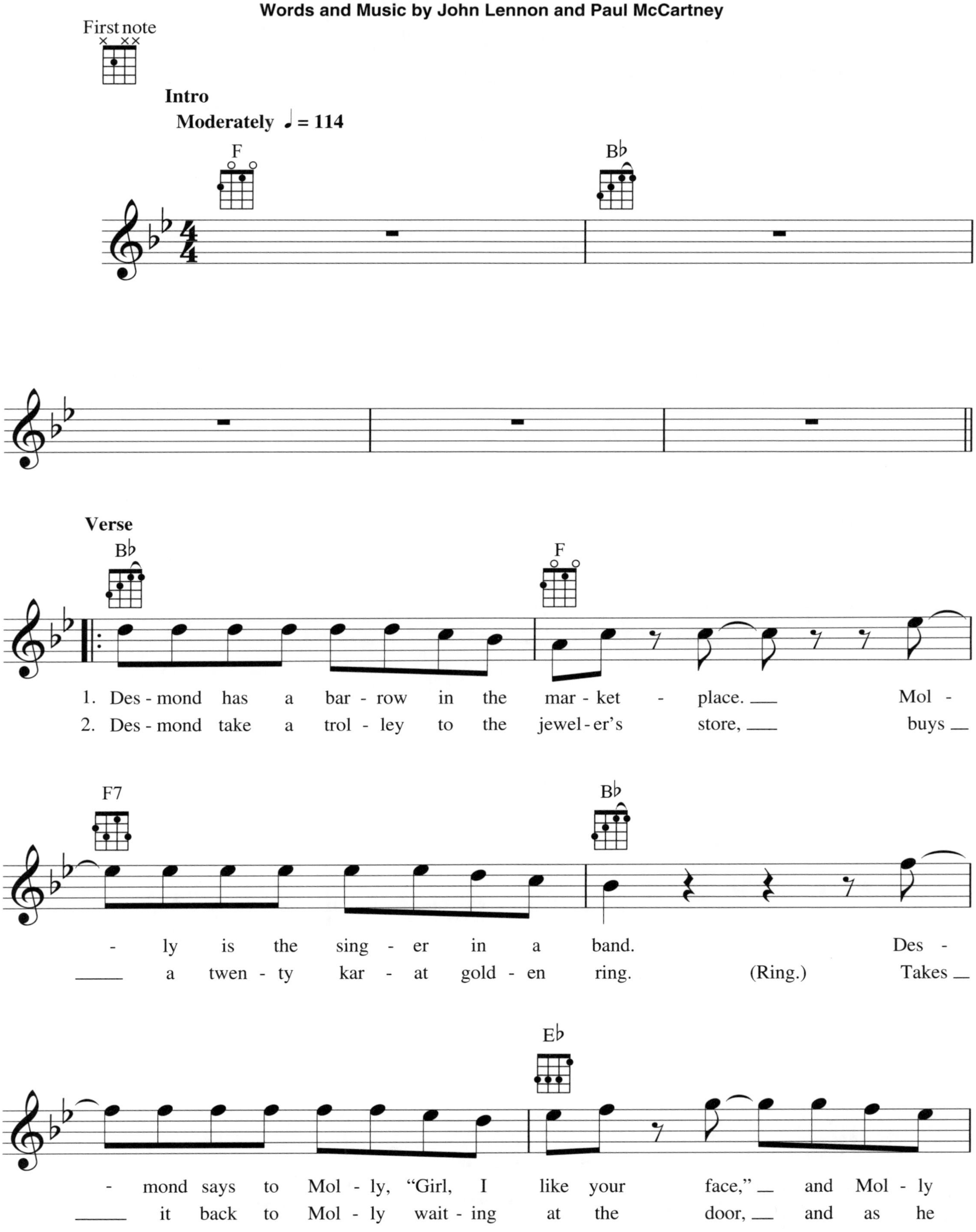

First note
Intro
Moderately ♩ = 114
F
B♭
Verse
B♭
F
1. Des - mond has a bar - row in the mar - ket - place. ___ Mol -
2. Des - mond take a trol - ley to the jewel - er's store, ___ buys ___
F7
B♭
- ly is the sing - er in a band. Des -
___ a twen - ty kar - at gold - en ring. (Ring.) Takes ___
E♭
- mond says to Mol - ly, "Girl, I like your face," ___ and Mol - ly
___ it back to Mol - ly wait - ing at the door, ___ and as he

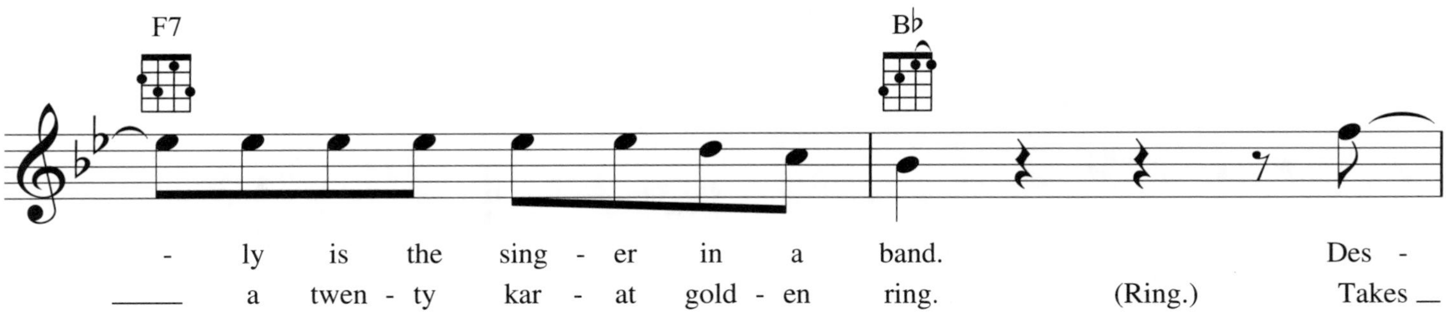

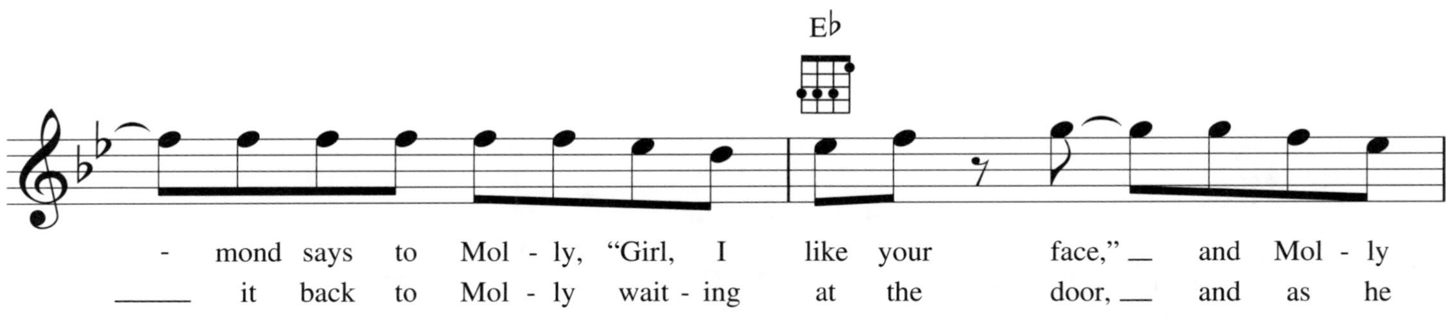

B♭ F B♭
says this as she takes him by the hand.
gives it to her she beg - ins to sing.
(Sing.)
Ob - la - di,

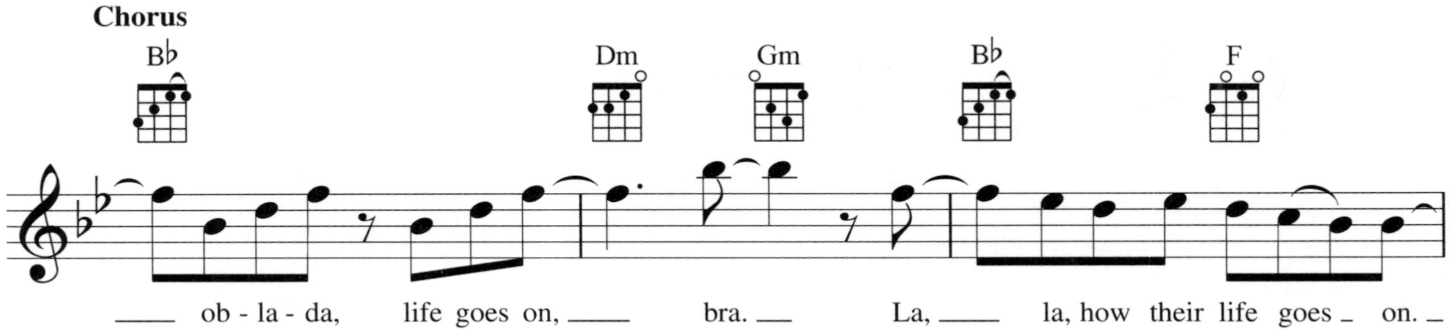
Chorus
B♭ Dm Gm B♭ F
ob - la - da, life goes on, bra. La, la, how their life goes on.

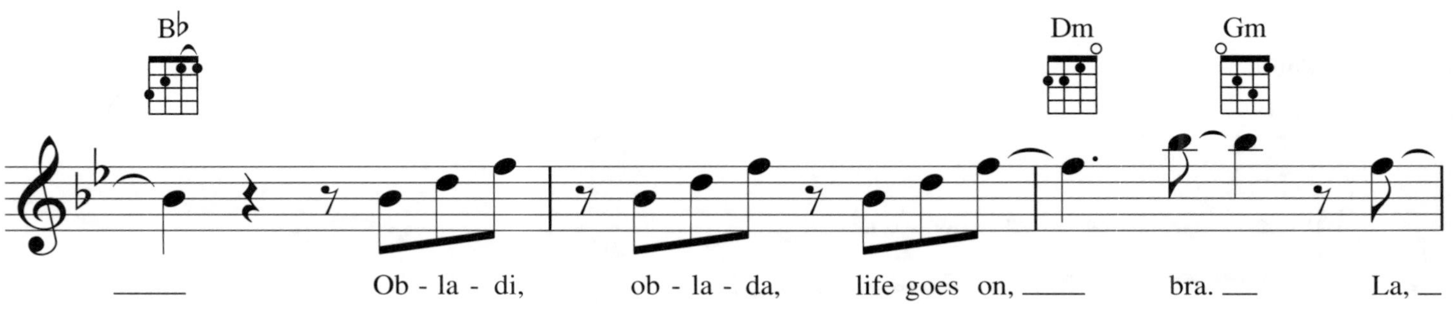
B♭ Dm Gm
Ob - la - di, ob - la - da, life goes on, bra. La,

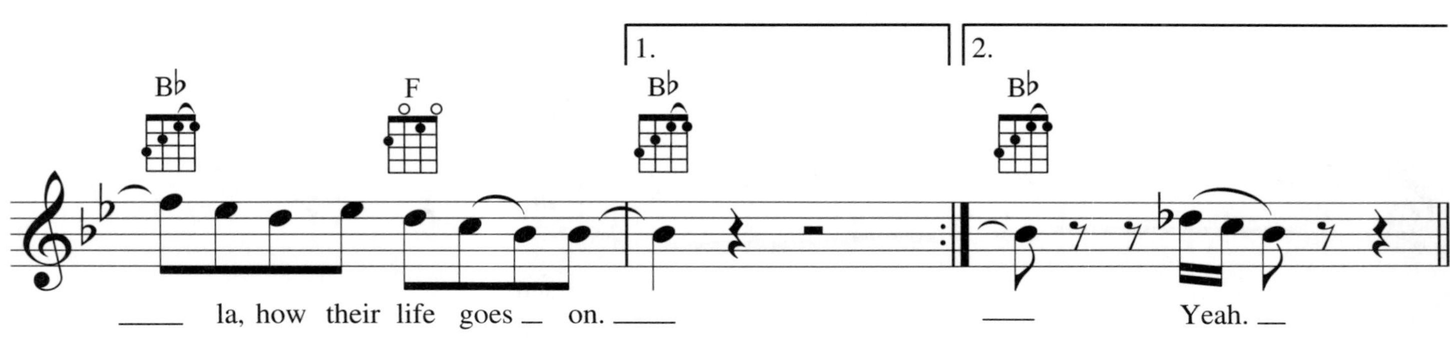
1. 2.
B♭ F B♭ B♭
la, how their life goes on. Yeah.

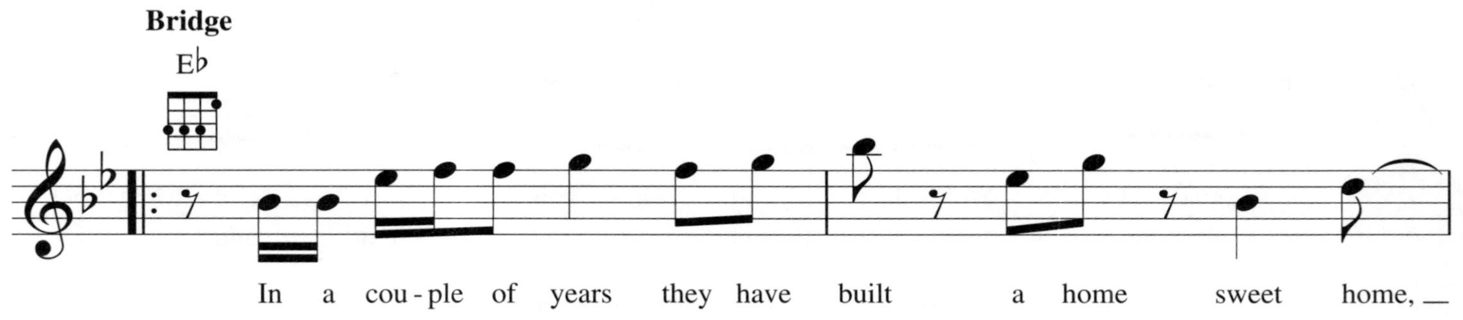
Bridge
E♭
In a cou - ple of years they have built a home sweet home,

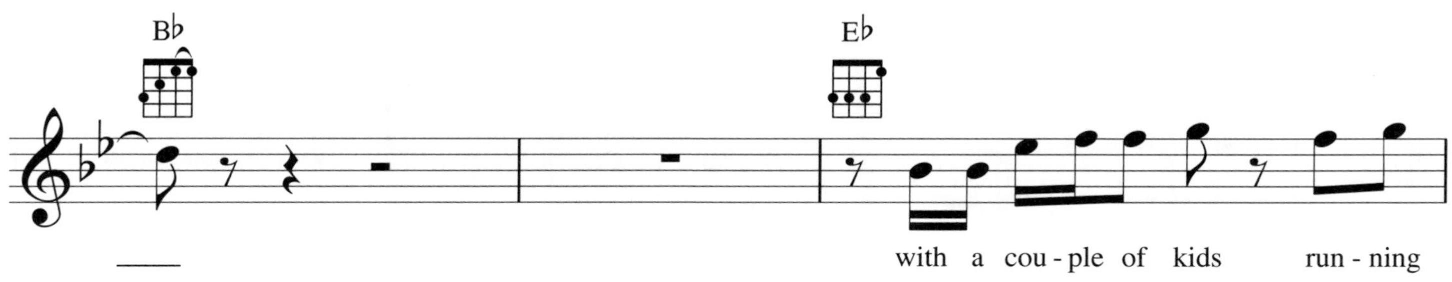
B♭
E♭
with a cou - ple of kids run - ning

B♭
F
in the yard of Des - mond and Mol - ly Jones.
4. Hey, hap -

Verse

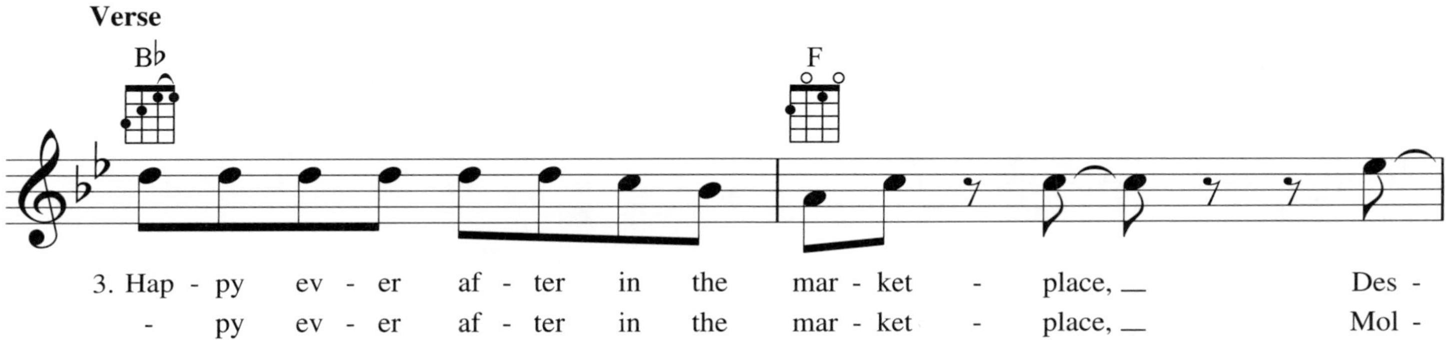
B♭
F
3. Hap - py ev - er af - ter in the mar - ket - place, Des -
- py ev - er af - ter in the mar - ket - place, Mol -

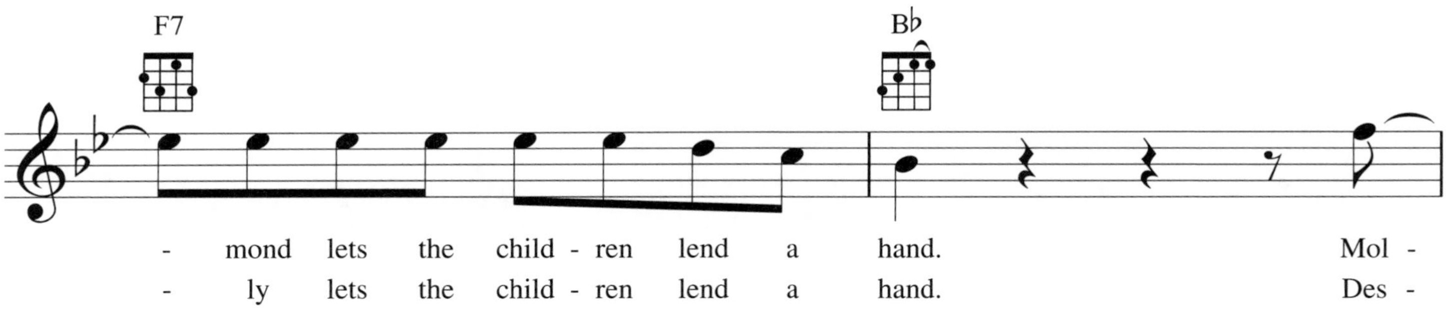
F7
B♭
- mond lets the child - ren lend a hand. Mol -
- ly lets the child - ren lend a hand. Des -

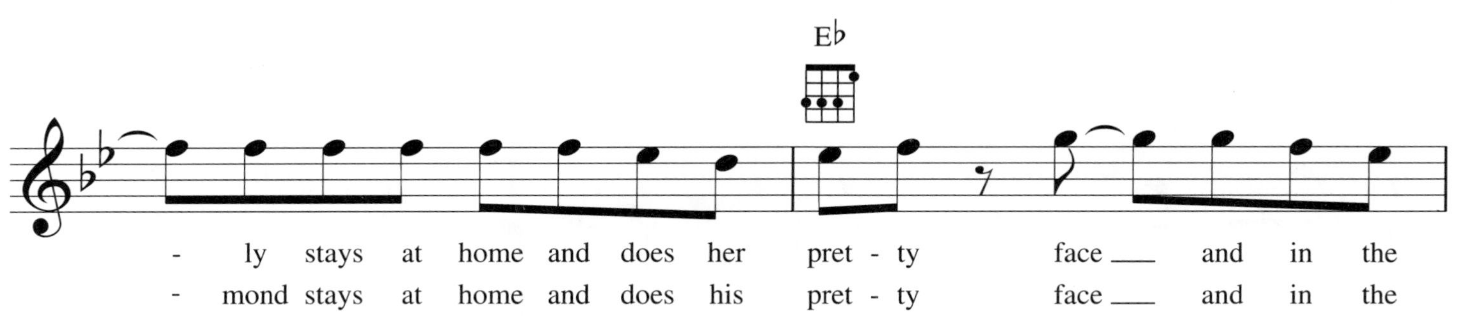
E♭
- ly stays at home and does her pret - ty face and in the
- mond stays at home and does his pret - ty face and in the

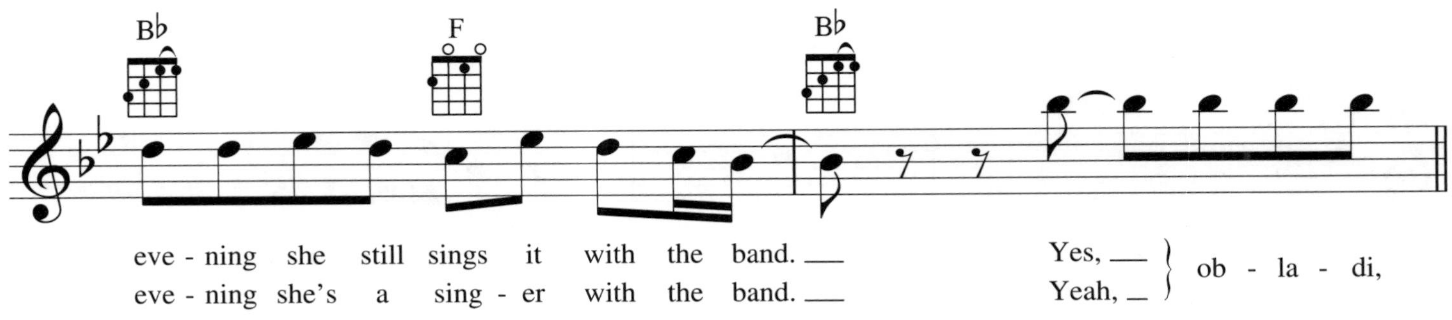

Chorus

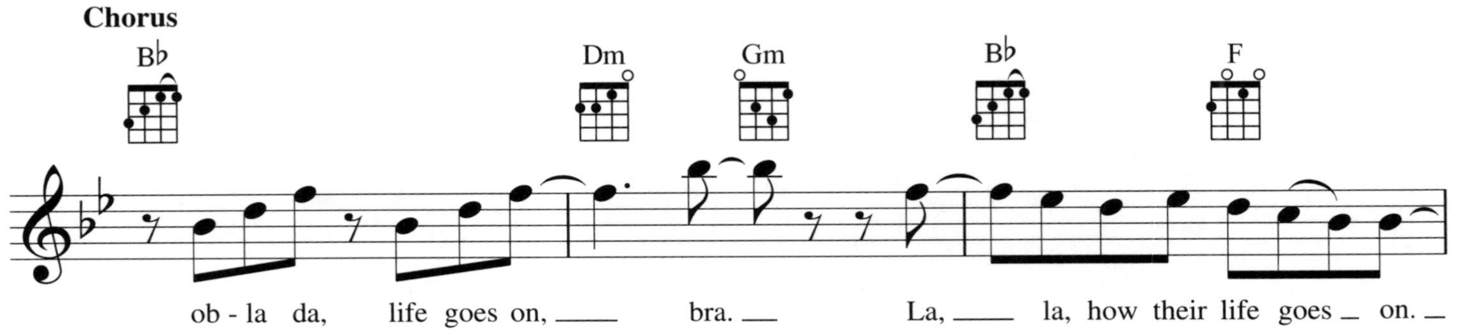

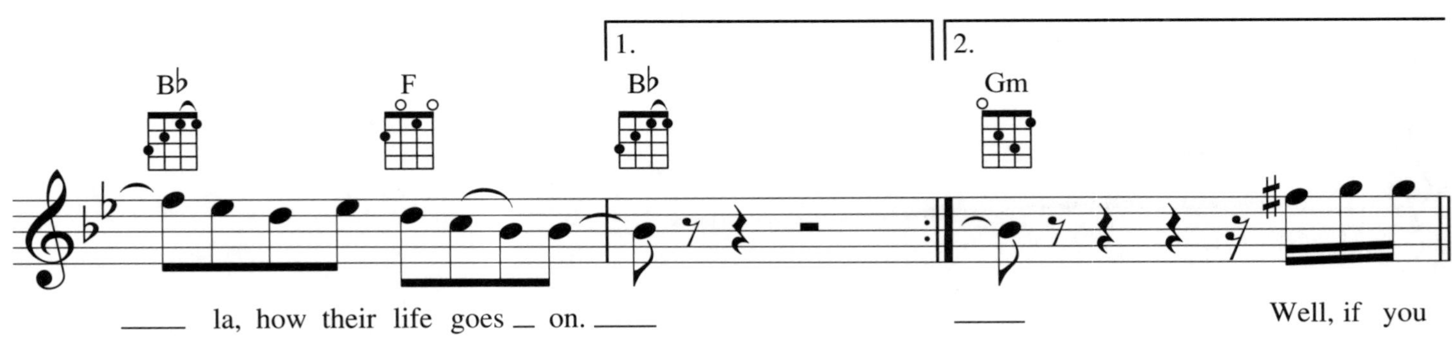

Outro

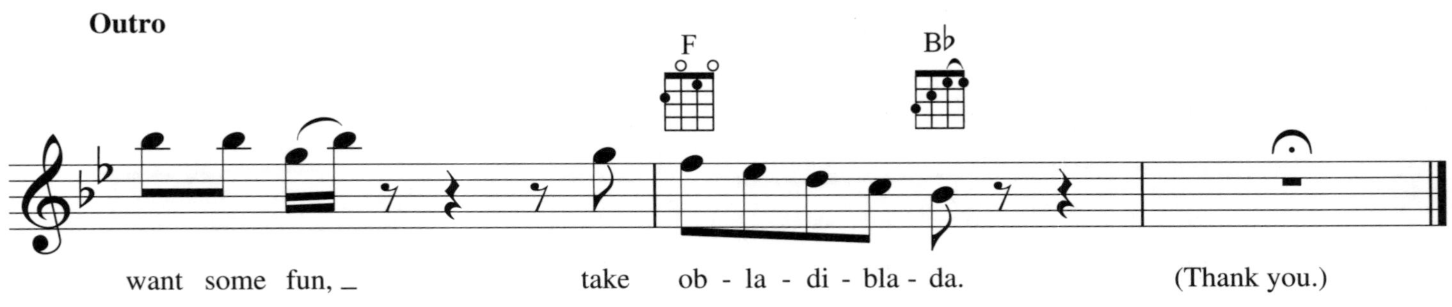

Penny Lane

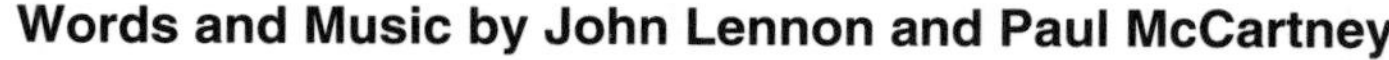

Words and Music by John Lennon and Paul McCartney

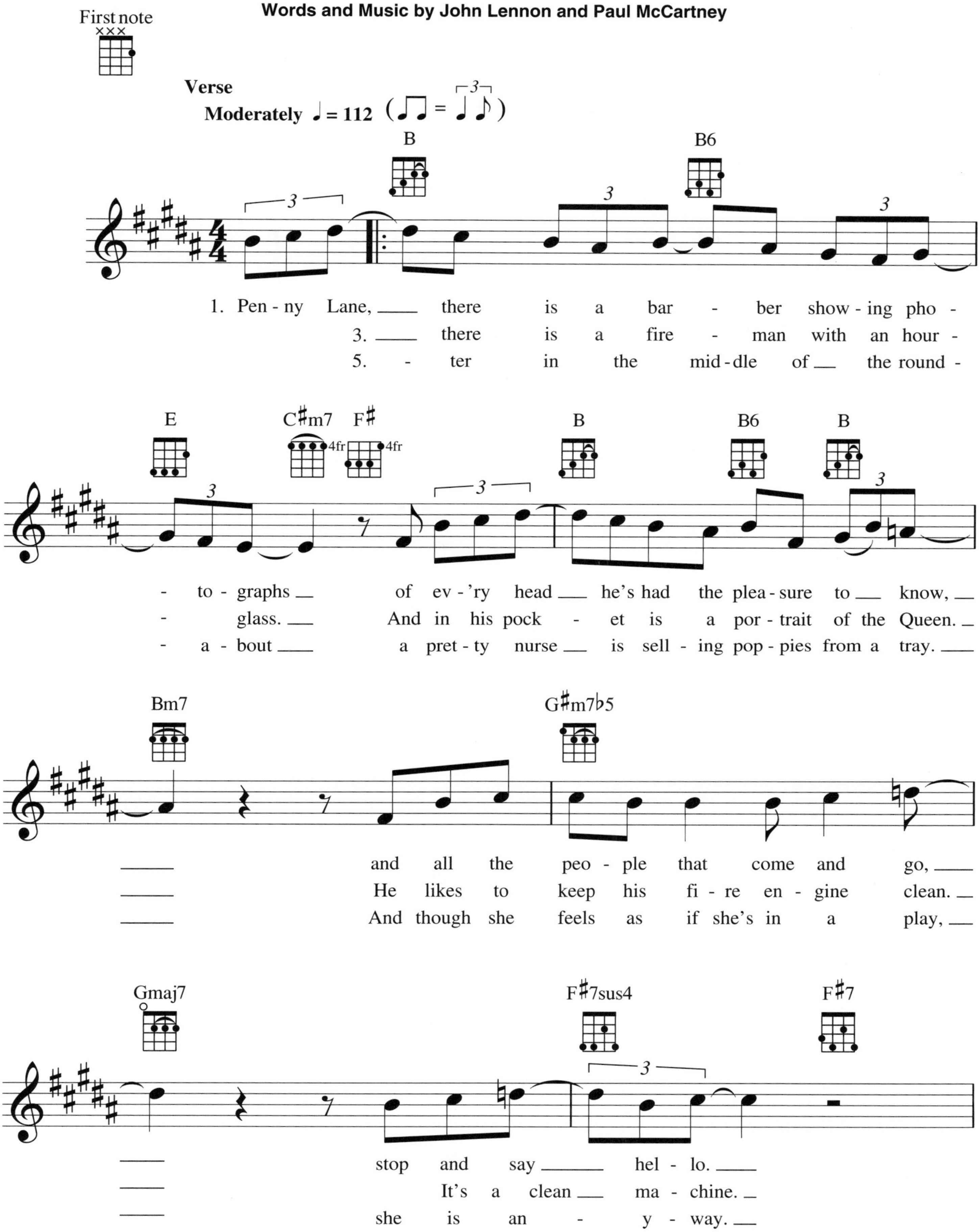
First note
Verse
Moderately ♩ = 112
B
B6
1. Pen - ny Lane, there is a bar - ber show - ing pho -
3. there is a fire - man with an hour -
5. - ter in the mid - dle of the round -
E
C♯m7
4fr
F♯
4fr
B
B6
B
- to - graphs of ev - 'ry head he's had the plea - sure to know,
- glass. And in his pock - et is a por - trait of the Queen.
- a - bout a pret - ty nurse is sell - ing pop - pies from a tray.
Bm7
G♯m7♭5
and all the peo - ple that come and go,
He likes to keep his fi - re en - gine clean.
And though she feels as if she's in a play,
Gmaj7
F♯7sus4
F♯7
stop and say hel - lo.
It's a clean ma - chine.
she is an - y - way.

Verse
F♯7sus4 F♯7 B B6 B
2. On the corner is a bank - er with a mo -
(Trumpet Solo) 4. Ah.
6. Pen - ny Lane, the bar - ber shaves an - oth - er cus -
E C♯m7 F♯ B B6 B
4fr 4fr
- tor car. The lit - tle chil - dren laugh at him be - hind his
Ah.
- tom - er. We see the bank - er sit - ting, wait - ing for a
Bm7 G♯m7♭5
back, and the bank - er nev - er wears a "mac"
Ah.
trim. Then the fi - re - man rush - es in
Gmaj7 F♯7sus4 F♯7
in the pour - ing rain,
Ah.
from the pour - ing rain,
Chorus
E A
ver - y strange.
ver - y strange.
Pen - ny Lane is in my ears

D
and in my eyes.
A
D
1., 3. There be - neath the blue sub - ur - ban skies I sit. And
2. Full of fish and fin - ger pies in sum - mer.
1., 2.
3.
F♯
4fr
mean - while back 3. in Pen - ny Lane
Mean - while back 5. be - hind the shel -
mean - while back, Pen - ny Lane
Chorus
B
E
is in my ears and in my eyes.
There, be - neath the blue sub - ur - ban skies.
Pen - ny Lane.
3

Ticket to Ride

Words and Music by John Lennon and Paul McCartney

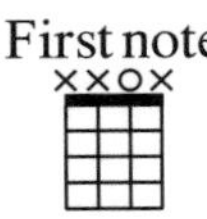

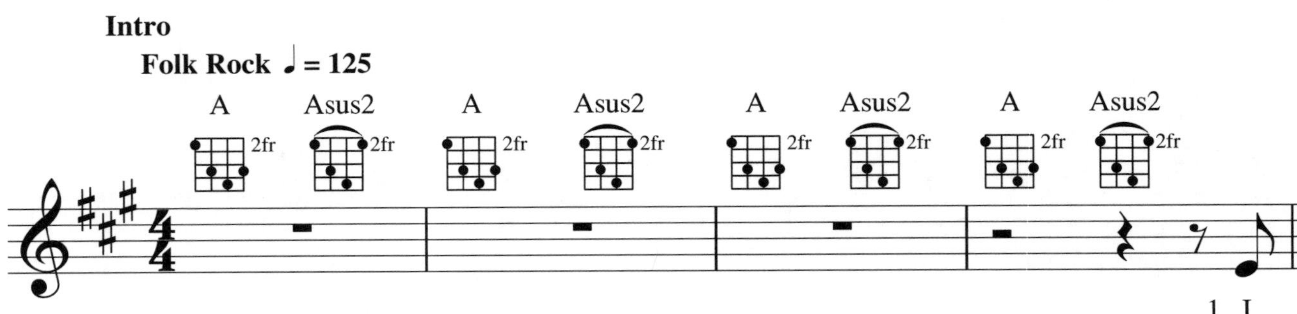

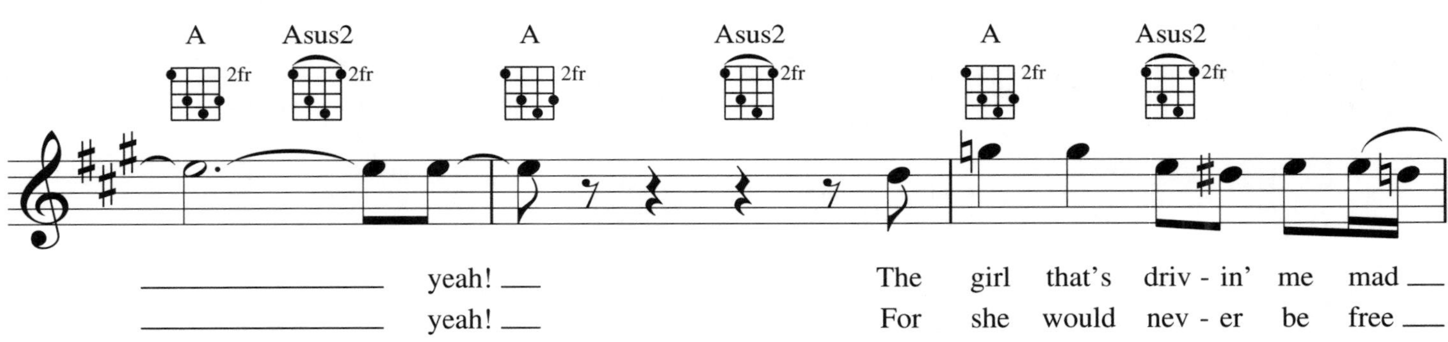

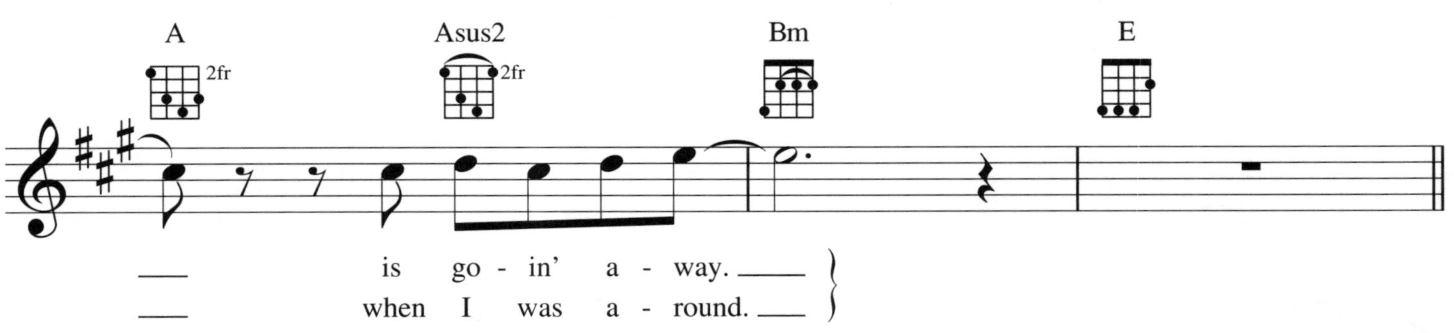

Chorus

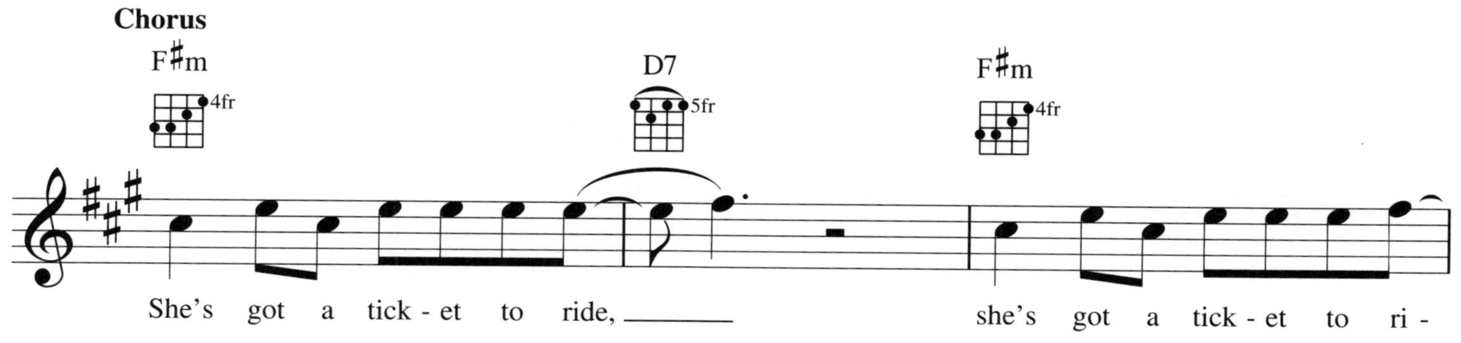
F♯m
4fr
D7
5fr
F♯m
4fr
She's got a tick - et to ride,
she's got a tick - et to ri -

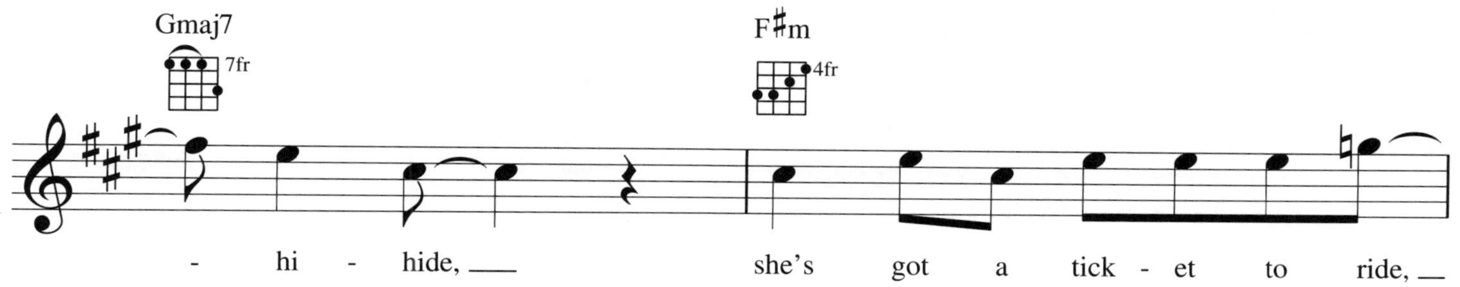
Gmaj7
7fr
F♯m
4fr
- hi - hide,
she's got a tick - et to ride,

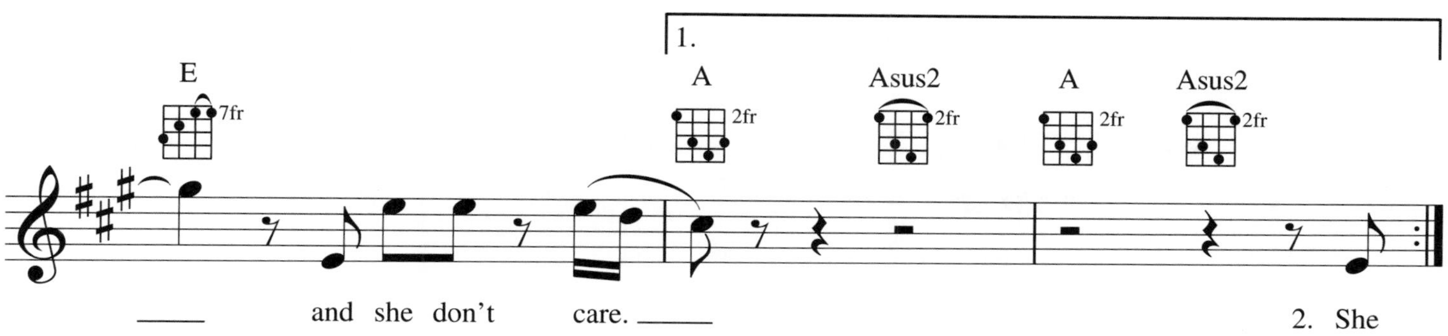
1.
E
7fr
A
2fr
Asus2
2fr
A
2fr
Asus2
2fr
and she don't care.
2. She

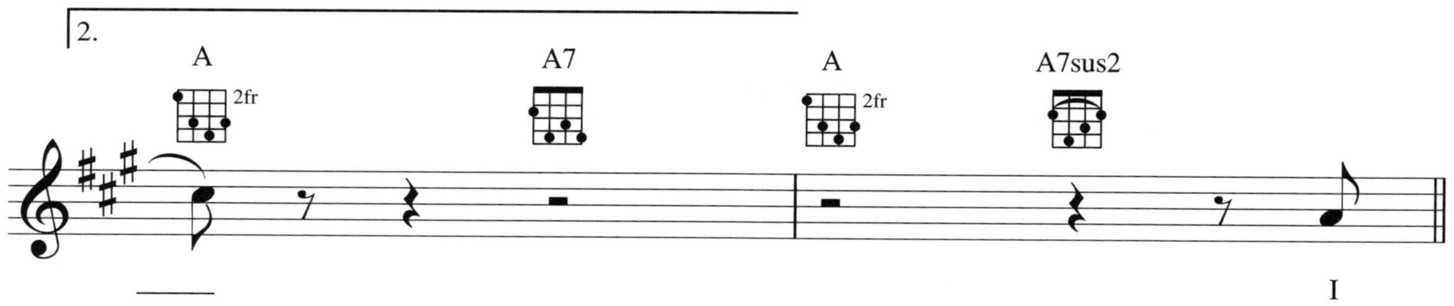
2.
A
2fr
A7
A
2fr
A7sus2
I

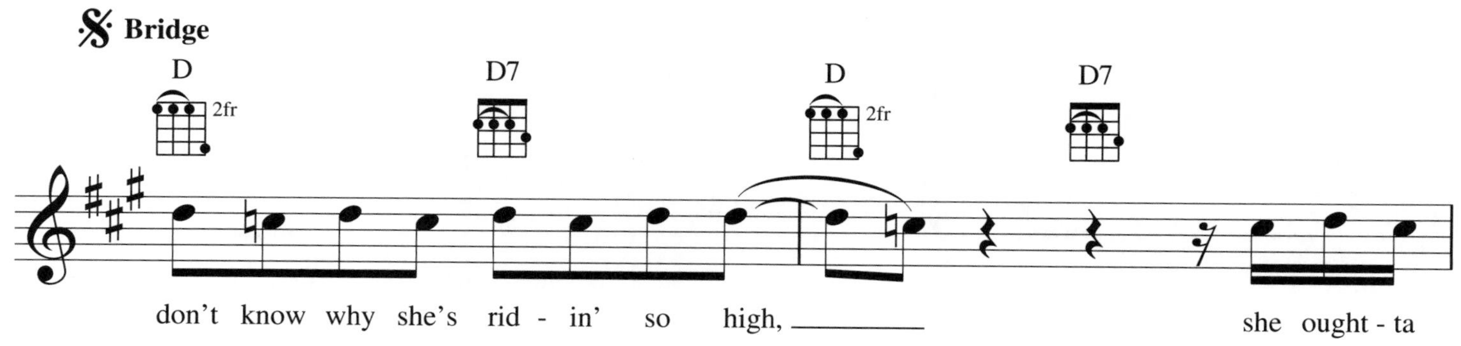
Bridge
D
2fr
D7
D
2fr
D7
don't know why she's rid - in' so high,
she ought - ta

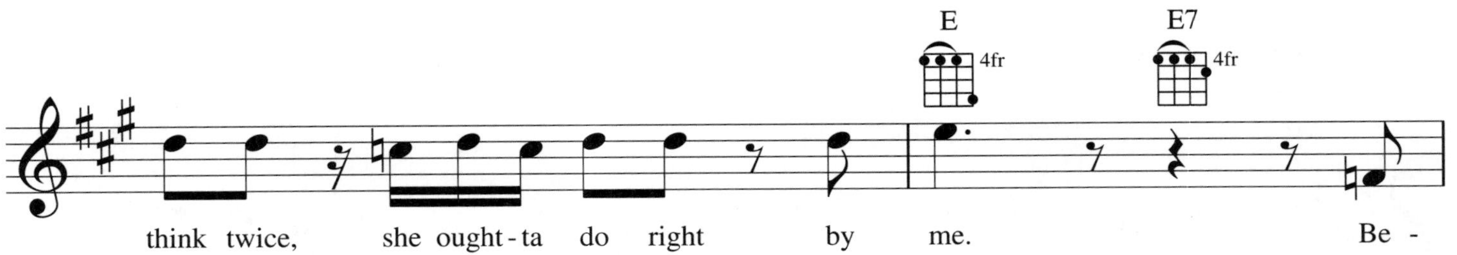
E
4fr
E7
4fr
think twice, she ought-ta do right by me. Be -

D
2fr
D7
D
2fr
D7
fore she gets to say - in' good - bye,
she ought - ta

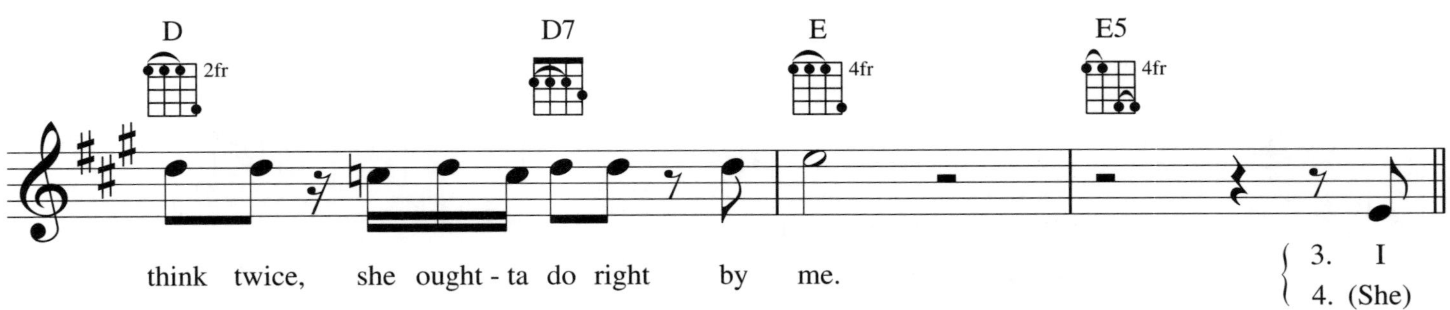
D
2fr
D7
E
4fr
E5
4fr
think twice, she ought - ta do right by me.
3. I
4. (She)

Verse
A
2fr
Asus2
2fr
A
2fr
Asus2
2fr
think I'm gon - na be sad, I think it's to - day,
said that liv - ing with me is bring - in' her down,

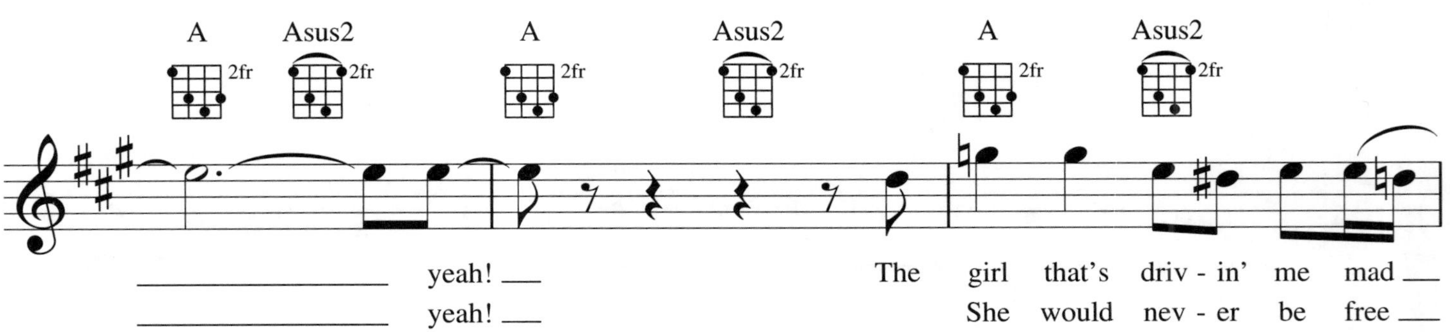
A
2fr
Asus2
2fr
A
2fr
Asus2
2fr
A
2fr
Asus2
2fr
yeah! The girl that's driv - in' me mad
yeah! She would nev - er be free

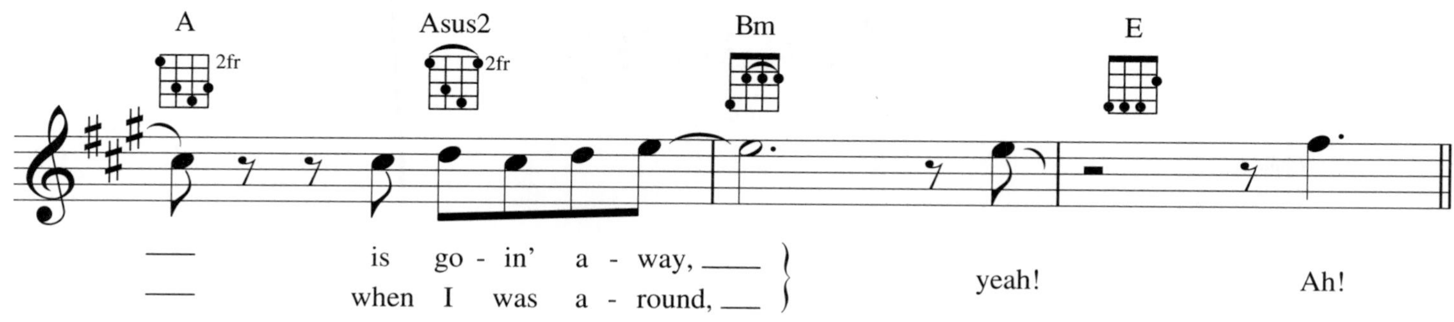
A
Asus2
Bm
E
is go - in' a - way,
when I was a - round,
yeah!
Ah!

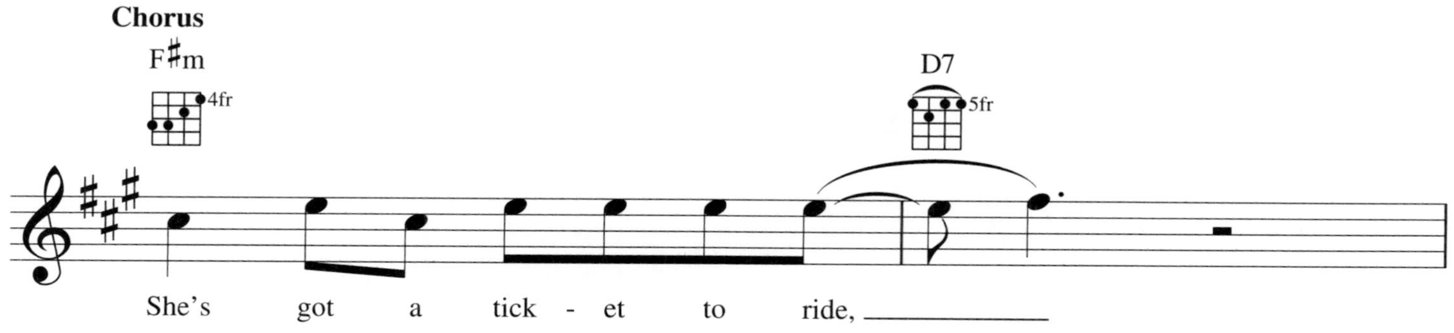
Chorus
F♯m
D7
She's got a tick - et to ride,

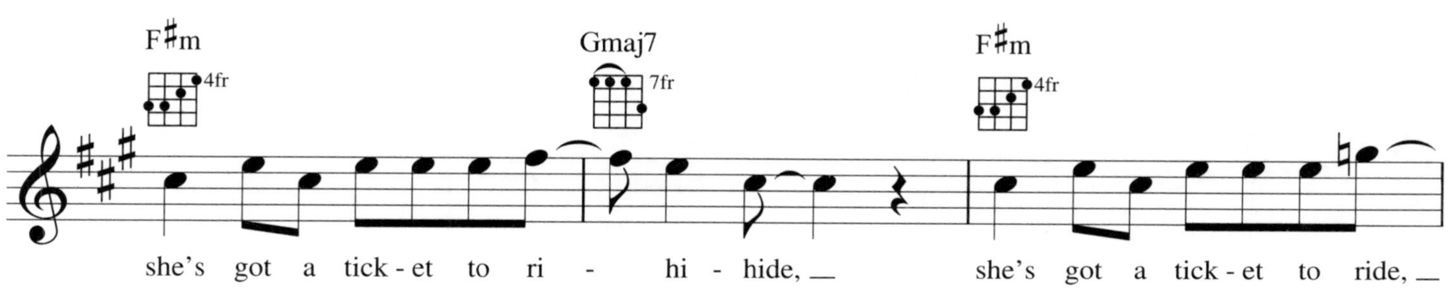
F♯m
Gmaj7
F♯m
she's got a tick - et to ri - hi - hide,
she's got a tick - et to ride,

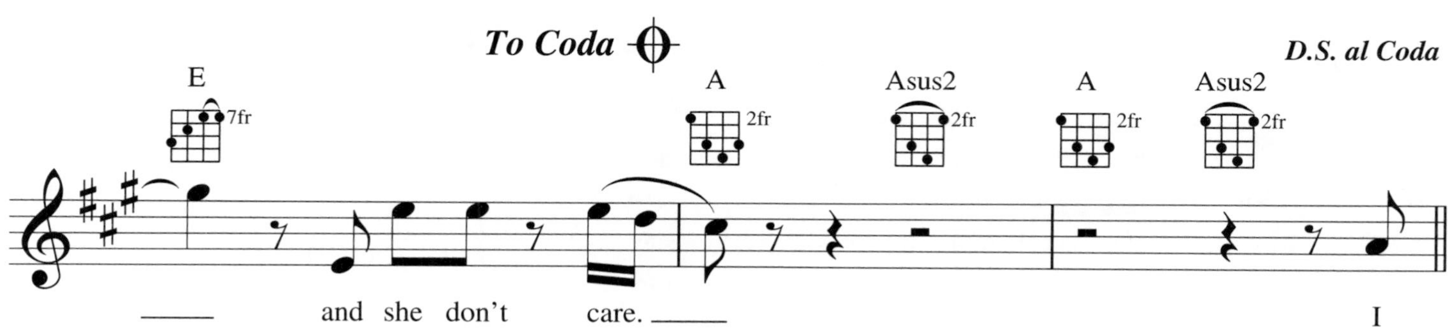
To Coda
D.S. al Coda
E
A
Asus2
A
Asus2
and she don't care.
I

Coda
Outro
Double-time feel
Repeat and fade
A
Asus2
N.C.
A
Asus2
A
Asus2
My ba - by don't care.
My ba - by don't

Yesterday

Words and Music by John Lennon and Paul McCartney

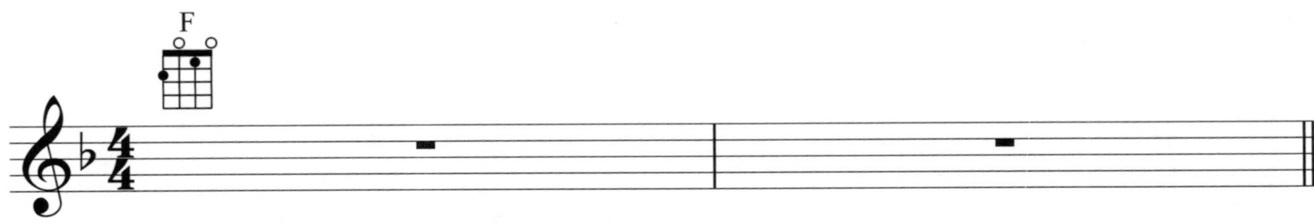

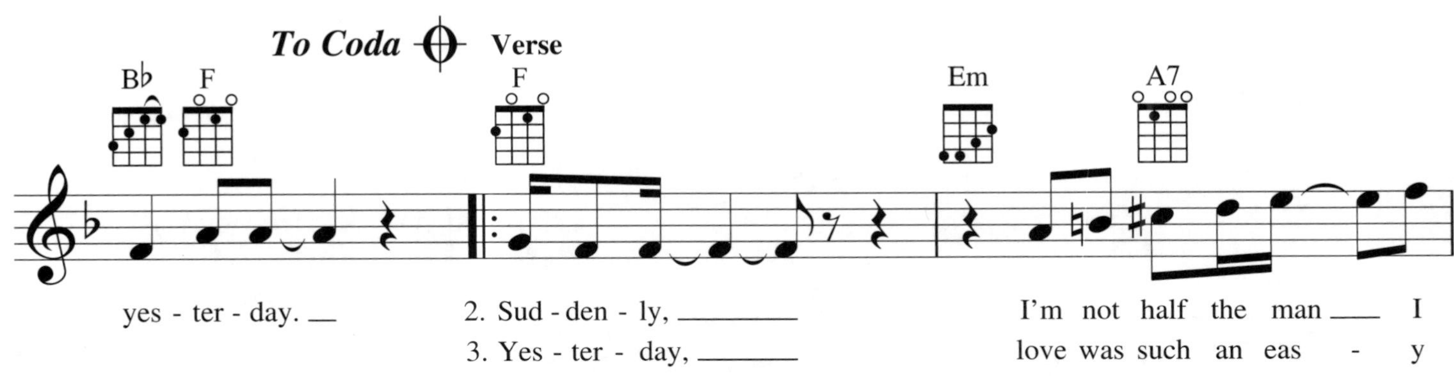

Dm
Bbmaj7
C7
F
Am
used to be. There's a shad - ow hang - ing o - ver me. Oh,
game to play. Now I need a place to hide a - way. Oh,
Dm7
G7
Bb
F
yes - ter - day came sud - den - ly.
I be - lieve in yes - ter - day.
Bridge
Em7(add11)
Em
A7
Dm
Am
Gm6
C7
Why she had to go, I don't know, she would - n't say.
F
Em
A7
Dm
Bb
Am
I said some - thing wrong, now I
1.
2.
D.S. al Coda
Gm6
C7
F
F
long for yes - ter - day. day.
Coda
F
G7
Bb
F
rit.
Hmm.

Yellow Submarine

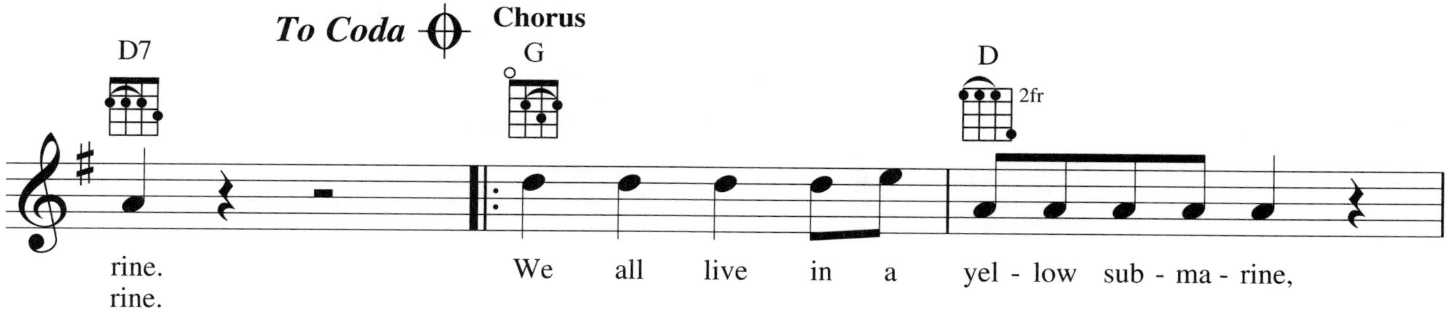
To Coda
Chorus
D7
G
D
2fr
rine.
rine.
We all live in a yel - low sub - ma - rine,

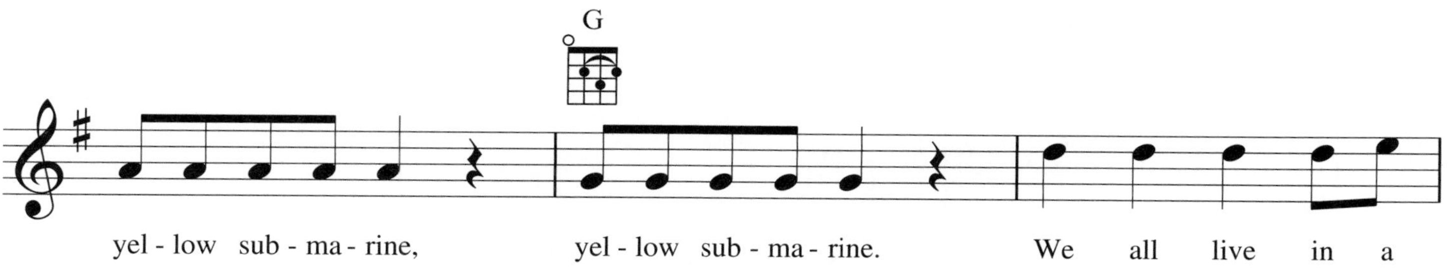
G
yel - low sub - ma - rine,
yel - low sub - ma - rine.
We all live in a

D
2fr
G
yel - low sub - ma - rine,
yel - low sub - ma - rine,
yel - low sub - ma - rine 2. And our friends

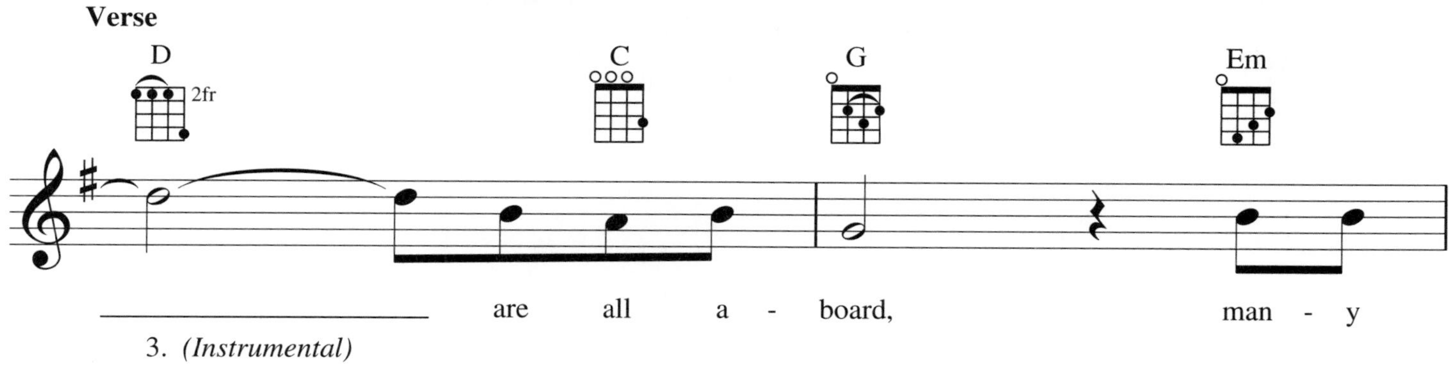
Verse
D
2fr
C
G
Em
are all a - board,
man - y
3. (Instrumental)

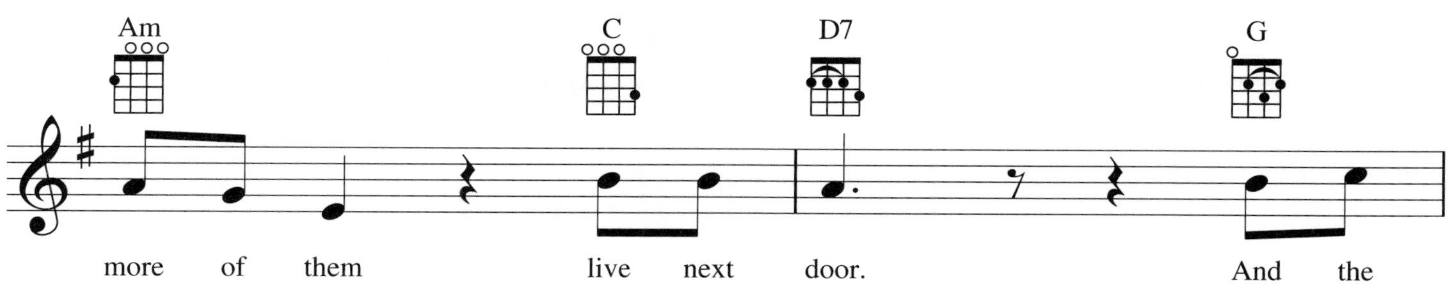
Am
C
D7
G
more of them live next door.
And the

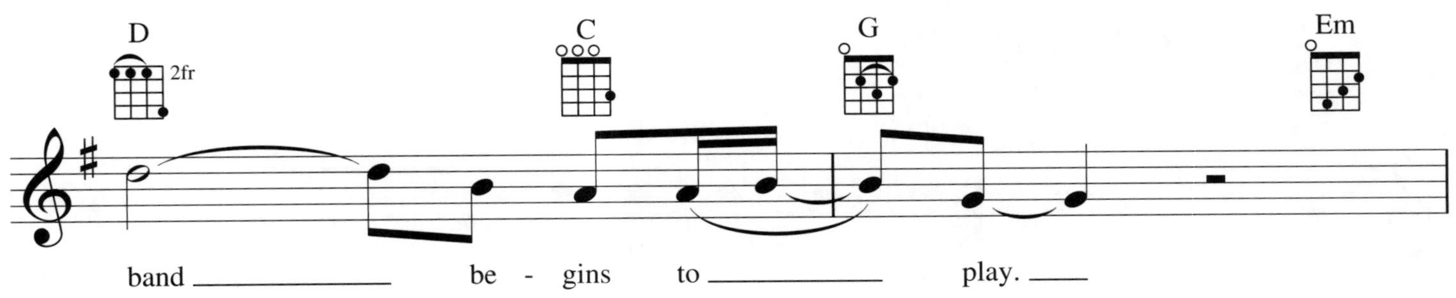
D
2fr
C
G
Em
band ___ be - gins to ___ play. ___

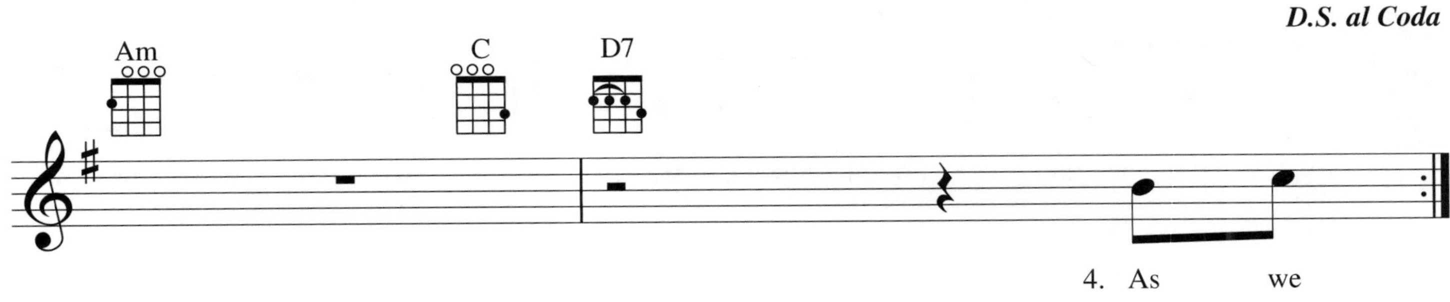
D.S. al Coda
Am
C
D7
4. As we

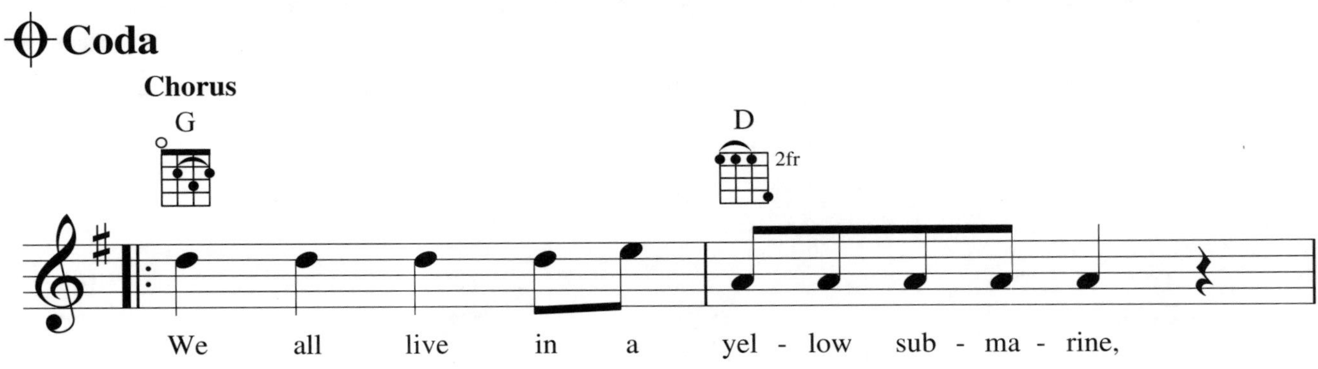
Coda
Chorus
G
D
2fr
We all live in a yel - low sub - ma - rine,

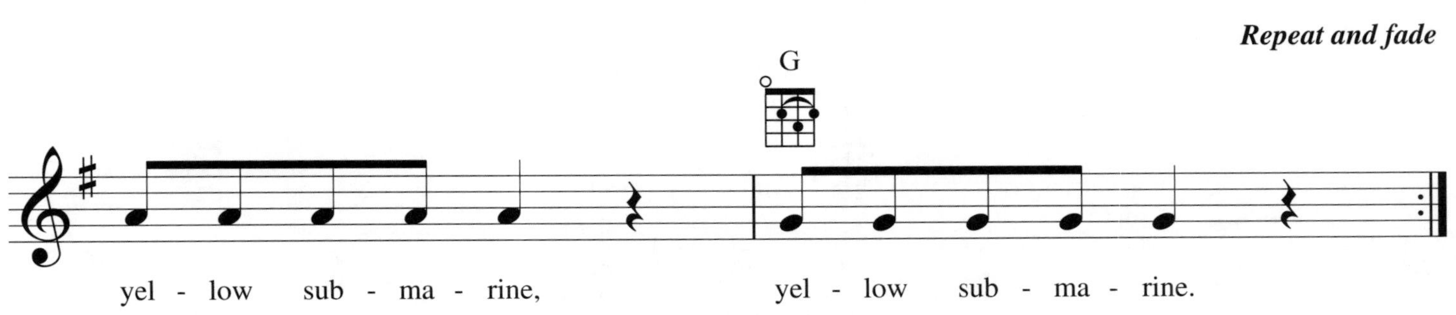
Repeat and fade
G
yel - low sub - ma - rine, yel - low sub - ma - rine.

Learn to play the Ukulele with these great Hal Leonard books!

Hal Leonard Ukulele Method

Book 1

by Lil' Rev

The Hal Leonard Ukulele Method is designed for anyone just learning to play ukulele. This comprehensive and easy-to-use beginner's guide by acclaimed performer and uke master Lil' Rev includes many fun songs of different styles to learn and play. The accompanying audio contains 46 tracks of songs for demonstration and play along. Includes: types of ukuleles, tuning, music reading, melody playing, chords, strumming, scales, tremolo, music notation and tablature, a variety of music styles, ukulele history and much more.

00695847 Book Only $8.99
00695832 Book/Online Audio $12.99
00320534 DVD $14.99

Book 2

00695948 Book Only $7.99
00695949 Book/Online Audio $11.99

Ukulele Chord Finder

00695803 9" x 12" $8.99
00695902 6" x 9" $7.99
00696472 Book 1 with Online Audio + Chord Finder $16.99

Ukulele Scale Finder

00696378 9" x 12" $8.99

Easy Songs for Ukulele

00695904 Book/Online Audio $16.99
00695905 Book $9.99

Ukulele for Kids

00696468 Book/Online Audio $14.99
00244855 Method & Songbook $22.99

Baritone Ukulele Method – Book 1

00696564 Book/Online Audio $12.99

Jake Shimabukuro Teaches Ukulele Lessons

Learn notes, chords, songs, and playing techniques from the master of modern ukulele! In this unique book with online video, Jake Shimabukuro will get you started on playing the ukulele. The book includes full transcriptions of every example, the video features Jake teaching you everything you need to know plus video of Jake playing all the examples.

00320992 Book/Online Video $22.99

Ukulele Aerobics

For All Levels, from Beginner to Advanced

by Chad Johnson

This package provides practice material for every day of the week and includes an online audio access code for all the workouts in the book. Techniques covered include: strumming, fingerstyle, slides, bending, damping, vibrato, tremolo and more.

00102162 Book/Online Audio $19.99

Fretboard Roadmaps – Ukulele

The Essential Patterns That All the Pros Know and Use

by Fred Sokolow & Jim Beloff

Take your uke playing to the next level! Tunes and exercises in standard notation and tab illustrate each technique. Absolute beginners can follow the diagrams and instruction step-by-step, while intermediate and advanced players can use the chapters non-sequentially to increase their understanding of the ukulele. The audio includes 59 demo and play-along tracks.

00695901 Book/Online Audio $15.99

All About Ukulele

A Fun and Simple Guide to Playing Ukulele

by Chad Johnson

If you wish there was a fun and engaging way to motivate you in your uke playing quest, then this is it: All About Ukulele is for you. Whether it's learning to read music, playing in a band, finding the right instrument, or all of the above, this enjoyable guide will help you.

00233655 Book/Online Audio $19.99

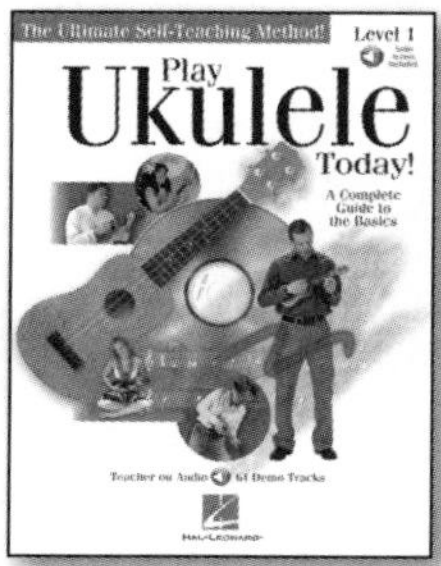

Play Ukulele Today!

A Complete Guide to the Basics

by Barrett Tagliarino

This is the ultimate self-teaching method for ukulele! Includes audio with full demo tracks and over 60 great songs. You'll learn: care for the instrument; how to produce sound; reading music notation and rhythms; and more.

00699638 Book/Online Audio $12.99
00293927 Book 1 & 2/Online Media $19.99

HAL•LEONARD®

www.halleonard.com

Prices, contents and availability subject to change without notice. Prices listed in U.S. funds.

0622
424